Actuarial mathematics of social security pensions

QUANTITATIVE METHODS IN SOCIAL PROTECTION SERIES
A series on financial, actuarial and statistical aspects of social security prepared jointly by the International Social Security Association and the Social Security Department of the International Labour Office

Modelling in health care finance: A compendium of quantitative techniques for health care financing
by Michael Cichon, William Newbrander, Hiroshi Yamabana, Axel Weber, Charles Normand, David Dror and Alexander Preker
ISBN 92-2-110862-7   1999

Actuarial mathematics of social security pensions
by Subramaniam Iyer
ISBN 92-2-110866-X   1999

Social budgeting
by Wolfgang Scholz, Krzysztof Hagemejer and Michael Cichon
ISBN 92-2-110861-9   2000

Actuarial practice in social security
by Pierre Plamondon, Anne Drouin, *et.al.*
ISBN 92-2-110863-5   2000

Other titles are in preparation

QUANTITATIVE METHODS IN
SOCIAL PROTECTION SERIES

Actuarial mathematics of social security pensions

Subramaniam Iyer

A joint technical publication of the
International Labour Office (ILO) and the
International Social Security Association (ISSA)

 International Labour Office • Geneva

Iyer, S.
Actuarial mathematics of social security pensions
Quantitative Methods in Social Protection Series
Geneva, International Labour Office/International Social Security Association, 1999
Actuarial valuation, social insurance, social security financing, method of financing, pension scheme, statistical method. 02.13.2

ISBN 92-2-110866-X

ILO Cataloguing-in-Publication data

FOREWORD

This book fills a gap in the actuarial literature. It deals with the application of actuarial principles and techniques to public social insurance pension schemes. Generally, these schemes are national in scope, mandatory and financed by contributions related to participants' earnings. Mature defined benefit public schemes are generally financed according to the pay-as-you-go system. Others, especially schemes in developing countries, adopt various levels of advance funding to finance the benefits.

Appropriate systems for financing public defined benefit pension schemes are widely debated. This volume contributes to the discussion by highlighting aspects where the financing of social security pensions differs from the funding of occupational pension schemes.

The book constitutes a ready reference for social security actuaries. While it is intended to serve as a textbook for persons engaged in actuarial work in social security institutions, it is of interest to other actuaries.

Subramaniam Iyer was commissioned to write the volume by the International Social Security Association. An Honorary Fellow of the Institute of Actuaries and a Member of the Swiss Association of Actuaries, he had a distinguished career with the Social Security Department of the International Labour Office from which he retired as Chief of the Financial, Actuarial and Statistical Branch. During his career, he acquired extensive expertise in the financing and actuarial valuations of social security pension schemes, particularly those in developing countries and in economies in transition.

This book is one of a series on financial, actuarial and statistical aspects of social security which is being prepared jointly by the International Social Security Association and the Social Security Department of the International Labour Office.

Colin Gillion, Director
Social Security Department
International Labour Office
Geneva, Switzerland

Dalmer D. Hoskins, Secretary General
International Social Security Association
Geneva, Switzerland

PREFACE

It is a privilege for me to have been asked by the International Social Security Association (ISSA) to write this book.

The book, I believe, provides a useful complement to the actuarial texts on pensions available in the English language. For while there is no dearth of text-books on the actuarial mathematics of occupational pensions, there does not appear to be any comparable volume on social security pensions.

Where social security pensions are financed on a pay-as-you-go basis, there is perhaps less scope for a sophisticated theoretical approach to the subject. It is, however, a historical fact that, in the early days of social security, social insurance pensions were financed according to an extension of the full-funding principle of occupational pensions. Although interest in funding waned over the years, the debate between the proponents of pay-as-you-go and funding is not over, and there has recently been a resurgence of interest in funding. At the present time, various levels of social security funding are practised by different countries, including full funding of defined contribution social security schemes.

The International Labour Office (ILO) has, over several decades, provided actuarial services to many national governments for the introduction or review of social security programmes. In the course of this work, which related largely to developing countries, but was more recently extended to Central and Eastern European transition economies, the ILO has developed new approaches and techniques. The ISSA, for its part, provided a valuable forum for discussing both the traditional and the innovative methodologies at the series of International Conferences of Social Security Actuaries and Statisticians. This book draws considerably from this rich actuarial material.

The book also aims at establishing a link between social security financing methods and occupational pension funding methods. This highlights the differences which exist between the two sets of methods, despite the inherent similarities. It is thus hoped that the book will be useful not only to social security actuaries, but also to actuaries specializing in occupational pensions for obtaining an understanding of the other field. However, it is not intended as a textbook on occupational pension funding, which is treated only in outline.

The introduction provides a brief description of the content of the book. The material is then presented in two parts. Part I, which deals with the theory, contains four chapters. Chapter 1 introduces the basic theory of the financing of social security pensions. This is followed by Chapter 2, which establishes the link with occupational pension funding. In Chapter 3, advanced topics related to social security pension financing are discussed. Chapter 4 is devoted to defined contribution schemes. The treatment in Part I throughout is on the basis of continuous functions, which helps to emphasize principles and interrelationships, and to elucidate the impact of different funding approaches.

Part II is concerned with techniques and comprises two chapters. Chapter 5 deals with the projection technique, which is ideally suited for the actuarial analysis of social security pensions. However, for the sake of completeness, the more traditional present value technique is included, in Chapter 6. In keeping with the practical nature of the subject-matter of Part II, the treatment is entirely in terms of discrete functions.

Six appendices complete the book. Appendix 1 provides a very brief summary of basic actuarial mathematics, to serve as a ready reference for readers. Appendix 2 illustrates the methods discussed in Chapters 1 and 2 with reference to a simple, hypothetical pension scheme. Appendix 3 is a glossary of the principal financing and funding methods, while Appendix 4 lists the various symbols used in the book. Appendices 5 and 6 contain further mathematical development of certain results stated in the text. Finally, a bibliography gives recognition to the many scientific papers and textbooks which were consulted during the preparation of the book.

This book is not a manual but a basic textbook. The reader will find here the principles underlying the mathematical theory and techniques of social security pensions, presented with reference to relatively simplified models. The actuarial practitioner will need to adapt this material to suit specific conditions and circumstances, and develop or acquire the necessary computer software for the purposes of practical application.

Acknowledgements

I would like to pay tribute to ILO and ISSA actuaries, both past and present, who, starting from the seminal papers of Anton Zelenka and Peter Thullen, have produced enough original material for a textbook such as this. I am particularly indebted to Dr. Thullen, whose 1973 manual on the actuarial techniques of social security (unfortunately not available in English) has been an invaluable source. I would refer the reader to this manual (in French) for greater detail on the more advanced aspects of social security pension financing.

I would like to express my gratitude to Warren McGillivray for the interest he took in this project and for his encouragement and support throughout the preparation of the book. It is fair to say that but for him, it would probably not have seen the light of day.

I could not have asked for a more distinguished panel of reviewers than Chris Daykin, Jean-Paul Picard and Michael Cichon. Had it not been for their thorough review and comments, the book would not have been what it is. I am, of course, responsible for any imperfections which still remain.

My thanks are also due to Alvaro Castro-Gutierrez, Anne Drouin, Kenichi Hirose, Denis Latulippe, Pierre Plamondon, Hiroshi Yamabana and Andrew Young for their helpful suggestions.

Despite my occasional neglect of domestic obligations, my wife and children cheerfully provided both moral and material support to me throughout the two years that I was engaged on this project. Harish Iyer gave technical advice for the computer processing of the book, and drew the graphs in Appendix 2. I thank my family for their help and understanding.

Subramaniam Iyer

CONTENTS

Contents

Contents

INTRODUCTION

This book is about *social security pension schemes*. These are institutionalized arrangements for the protection of the aged, the disabled, and dependants who lose their breadwinner through death, which are set up at the national level through government initiative. The provisions of such a scheme are laid down in legislation; these cover, in particular, the rights and obligations of all individuals and establishments affected by the scheme, including the contributions to be paid and the benefits to be received. Such a scheme is usually mandatory for specified categories of the population (e.g. some or all employed persons, some or all economically active persons, all residents). It is administered directly by a government department or agency or by an autonomous parastatal organization subject to government supervision. The scheme's solvency and ability to pay future benefits is, in most cases, guaranteed, implicitly or explicitly, by the government.

Statutory social security pension schemes are complemented by *private pension schemes* which may provide "top-up" benefits or may be accepted as alternatives to the national scheme if members of such schemes are allowed to "contract out" of it. Private schemes often take the form of *occupational pension schemes*, which are sponsored by individual employers or groups of employers, or they may be organized as mutual funds or commercially run funds. There are also other voluntary arrangements, such as *personal pension policies* and *annuity policies* issued by insurance companies.

Both social security pension schemes and occupational pension schemes may take one of two different forms: *defined benefit* or *defined contribution*. Essentially the difference is that, in the former case, the benefit formula is specified and the financing arrangements – including, in particular, the contributions payable – are determined as the amounts needed to finance the benefits; in the latter, the contributions to be paid are specified, and the benefits are what result from investing these specified contributions.

This book is mainly concerned with social security pension schemes of the defined benefit type, but consideration is also given to defined contribution

1

social security schemes. It is assumed that the reader is familiar with the general structure of such schemes. A summary description is provided below of the design features of these schemes and the common variations which arise in practice; reference may be made to other sources for more details (e.g. ILO, 1984). The book refers to retirement benefits of occupational pension schemes for comparison purposes but does not discuss other private scheme benefits. Accordingly, no description of the benefit structure of these schemes is provided, but the interested reader may refer to other specialized publications (e.g. Lee, 1986).

DEFINED BENEFIT SOCIAL SECURITY PENSION SCHEMES

Sources of finance

The sources of finance of social security pension schemes may include one or more of the following: *contributions* paid by the individuals covered by the scheme; contributions paid by the employers on behalf of covered employed persons; government subsidies and earmarked taxes.

Contributions may be *flat rate* or *earnings related*. In the context of earnings-related contributions, "earnings" may refer not to total earnings but only to earnings up to a specified ceiling, above a specified threshold or between two levels. Contribution rates may be uniform or may vary according to the level of earnings (system of wage-classes).

Qualifying conditions for pensions

The contingencies or risks covered by defined benefit social security pension schemes include *retirement* on attainment of a particular age, inability to continue working on account of *invalidity*, and *death* while in active status or when in receipt of a retirement or invalidity pension.

Retirement pensions are normally subject to retirement from active employment, the attainment of a specified age and the satisfaction of a specified minimum qualifying period. A lower pensionable age may apply to females relative to males, or to particular classes of members. Retirement with a normal scale pension at an earlier age may be permitted in certain cases, for example, for persons engaged in arduous or unhealthy work or for those considered to be prematurely aged. Voluntary retirement at an earlier age with a reduced pension may be allowed, subject to qualifying service conditions being satisfied.

The qualifying period usually refers to calendar periods of contribution but, depending on the scheme, may refer to periods of insurance, employment or residence (for consistency, the term *insurance period* will be used below). Periods of incapacity for work due to sickness, maternity or employment injury, or of child-rearing or caring for an invalid, may be assimilated to insurance periods. When a new pension scheme is introduced, transitional provisions may provide for a lower qualifying period for the initial entrants above a certain age. Sometimes a contribution density condition, that is, the credit of a minimum service period per year of membership, may also be required to be satisfied.

Invalidity pensions are, in the first instance, subject to the condition of existence of at least a specified degree of invalidity according to an adopted definition, which could be based on one of three concepts: *physical, occupational* or *general invalidity*. Physical invalidity refers to the loss of a bodily part or of a physical or mental faculty; occupational invalidity refers to the loss of earning capacity in the previous occupation; general invalidity refers to the loss of the capacity to carry out any remunerative activity. The minimum degree of invalidity to qualify usually varies from one-half to two-thirds. In addition, a qualifying period – considerably shorter than that required for retirement pensions – or a contribution density condition is generally imposed.

Survivors' pensions are provided to specified dependants (mainly widows/widowers and orphans), subject to the condition that either the deceased insured person would have qualified for an invalidity pension had he or she claimed such a pension on the date of death or was already in receipt of a retirement or invalidity pension. The widow may be required to satisfy further conditions such as having attained a specified minimum age, being disabled or having the care of young children. The widow's pension often ceases on her remarriage, sometimes with the payment of a lump-sum remarriage grant. The orphan's pension is discontinued on attaining a specified age but may be extended under certain circumstances, for example if the child is pursuing full-time education or is disabled.

When the insurance period is not sufficient to qualify for a retirement, invalidity or survivors' pension, a lump-sum grant may be provided.

The pension formula

The pension formula can be either *flat rate* or *earnings related*. (In what follows, the word *salary* is used interchangeably with *earnings*.) A flat-rate formula provides for pensions which are uniform in amount, regardless of the level of the individual's earnings, while an earnings-related formula links the pension to the previous salary of the individual. *Earnings* refer to the insured salary, which may be different from the actual salary due to the application of a threshold and/or a ceiling. A mixed formula is also possible, with flat-rate and earnings-related elements.

With earnings-related pensions, the basis of calculation may be the *final*, the *final average* or the *career average* insured salary of the individual. The final average is typically computed over the last one to five years of the career. Where the career average basis is used, the component salaries entering into the computation of the average may be indexed to compensate for the rise in the general level of earnings up to the time of the award of the pension.

The *replacement rate*, that is, the pension amount as a percentage of the salary used as the basis of calculation will, in an earnings-related scheme, typically consist of the sum of a flat percentage independent of the length of the insurance period and a variable percentage linked to the insurance period. A maximum percentage is usually prescribed for the replacement rate. The same type of pension formula will generally apply to retirement, invalidity and survivors' pensions. Minimum and maximum pensions may be prescribed in absolute terms (i.e. in monetary units).

In the case of entrants who are over a specified age when a scheme is started, special credits of insurance periods, increasing by age, may be awarded to compensate for their inability to complete a full insurance record. For invalidity pensions, special credits, decreasing by age, may be awarded to compensate for the loss of potential future insurance periods; by extension, these credits may also apply to survivors' pensions arising from the death of active insured persons.

The survivors' pension calculated according to the pension formula is usually allocated to individual survivors according to prescribed percentages, subject to the total of all the shares not exceeding 100 per cent of the global survivors' pension.

Indexation of pensions

The legislation may provide for a *systematic* or *automatic* adjustment of pensions, that is, it may lay down the procedure and the method of adjustment; or for *adjustment in principle* only, in which case a regular review may be required without specifying how any increase is to be determined. Where the legislation does not contain any provision on indexation, ad hoc adjustment may be provided from time to time by the concerned authorities. The mechanism of indexation may be based on the cost-of-living index, an index of earnings, or some mixture of the two, and limits may apply to the extent of adjustment either in absolute terms or as a proportion. Indexation should normally also apply to parameters expressed in monetary units, such as earnings thresholds or ceilings and maximum and minimum pension amounts.

DEFINED CONTRIBUTION SOCIAL SECURITY SCHEMES

One type of defined contribution social security scheme is a *national provident fund*. An individual account is opened in the name of each member of the provident fund, in which the member's (and, if applicable, the employer's) contributions are registered. There is usually no state contribution or subsidy. Interest is added from time to time to the account. The accumulated balance is generally paid as a lump sum on retirement, attainment of invalidity or death before retirement. Death after retirement is not a directly covered contingency. An option to convert the lump-sum benefit into an annuity is sometimes available. Partial withdrawals from the account may also be permitted for other purposes, particularly for the purchase of residential property, education of children or health care expenses.

The Chilean social security reform of 1981 gave rise to another type of defined contribution scheme, which is referred to as a *mandatory retirement savings* scheme. Such a scheme, although statutory, is administered by private companies which are subject to government supervision. Contributions are paid by the members only. Individual accounts are maintained as in national provident funds, but schemes are required to guarantee a minimum rate of interest. On retirement of a member, the accumulated balance is mandatorily converted into an indexed pension subject to a specified minimum which is guaranteed by the State. Invalidity and survivors' benefits are provided through separate insurance arrangements (for details see Gillion and Bonilla, 1992).

There are also hybrid schemes, such as those based on the "points system", where there is a defined benefit but it is calculated by a formula which derives from the contributions paid. Monetary contributions are converted into points based on the value of the point when the contribution is made; the pension, which depends on the total number of accumulated points, is in turn converted back into monetary units based on the value of the point at the time of payment.

Another hybrid is the "notional defined contribution scheme", where contributions are credited to individual accounts but used to pay current pensions. The notional balances in the accounts are credited annually with a growth factor (e.g. real wage growth, growth in gross domestic product), and at retirement the notional balances are converted into pensions. The scheme is unfunded, while the benefit is based on an individual account accumulation as in a traditional defined contribution scheme. During the accumulation period it closely resembles a career average, adjusted earnings, defined benefits scheme (McGillivray, 1997).

PART I

THEORY

THE FINANCING OF SOCIAL SECURITY PENSIONS

1

1.1 INTRODUCTION

When a pension scheme is set up, one of the major questions to be resolved is the method of financing the scheme. By this is meant the arrangement according to which resources will be raised to meet the expenditures (on benefits, and possibly on administration as well) under the scheme, as they arise. In other words, this refers to the system governing the amount and timing of the contributions to the scheme. As will be seen later, there are several different methods by which a given pension scheme may be financed.

This chapter first identifies the basic demographic and economic parameters which affect, on the one hand, a pension scheme's expenditures and, on the other, the insured salaries of the covered population on which the contributions to the scheme are generally based. It then discusses the characteristic trend over time of these financial aggregates and enunciates the basic mathematical principles of financing. It next addresses the special considerations which arise with social security pension schemes and presents the main financial systems employed in this area. The corresponding discussion of occupational pension schemes is the subject of Chapter 2.

The initial analysis will refer to a new pension scheme rather than to an ongoing scheme. This will permit a view of the whole spectrum of its financial evolution over time. Further, in order to simplify the treatment, the discussion is based on a highly simplified model of reality. It is assumed that a projection has been made, at the outset, of the future financial aggregates and that the experience will conform exactly to the initial expectation. On this basis, the different financing methods which may be applied to the scheme are discussed. This forward planning approach highlights the long-term financial implications of a pension scheme.

The reality, however, is much more complex. In particular, it is highly unlikely that the projection made at the outset of the scheme will be exactly realized. In fact, it should be expected that the projection exercise will be repeated at intervals, and adjustments or refinements made from time to time to the financing method under application. These practical aspects are taken up in Part II of this book.

In order to concentrate on essentials, the analysis will refer mainly to a scheme with a pension formula which is strictly proportional to the period of contributory membership and the final salary of the insured person. Moreover, attention will be focused on retirement pensions. These restrictions do not, however, invalidate the wider applicability of the theory which is developed. The extension of the principles to invalidity and survivors' pensions is considered in Chapter 3.

The terms "contributions" and "contribution rate" refer to the total resources allocated to the scheme by all the contributing parties, including the employer, the covered employee and possibly the State as well.

1.2   THE BASIC DEMOGRAPHIC AND ECONOMIC PARAMETERS

The future course of a retirement pension scheme is determined, in the first instance, by the demographic and economic characteristics of the population initially covered. Further, it is determined by a series of factors, demographic and economic, which will be experienced by the scheme over its lifetime. In general, these parameters will vary over time. For the present purposes, however, it is assumed that they maintain a constant, positive value. They include, in particular:

- the force of interest: δ
- the force of growth of new entrants: ρ
- the force of escalation of insured salaries: γ
- the force of pension indexation: β
- the (age-specific) forces of mortality, invalidity and other decrements: μ_x^d, μ_x^i, and so on.

In addition, the force of inflation is denoted by θ.

The parameter γ refers to the instantaneous rate at which the general level of salaries is growing. This is on top of the progression of individual salaries due to age/seniority, called the salary scale.

There are certain relationships which should hold between these factors. Barring exceptional circumstances (for example, during major economic transition) the rate of salary escalation should ideally be expected to exceed the rate of inflation, the difference representing the gain in productivity. Pension indexation should be expected to at least maintain the purchasing power of pensions (*price indexation*) but might even maintain the standard of living of pensioners on a par with that of active insured persons (*wage indexation*). Symbolically, $\gamma \geq \beta \geq \theta$.

Further, in the long run, the rate of interest should be expected to exceed the sum of the rate of growth of the insured population and the rate of salary escalation. This relationship has particular economic significance (Aaron, 1966). It is therefore assumed that $\delta > \rho + \gamma$.

Another factor which is relevant to social security pension schemes is the average "density of contributions", which indicates the proportion of the potential time that members in the active age range are effectively in contributory service. For the present purposes this factor is assumed uniformly at 100 per cent; the effect of alternative density assumptions is considered in Chapter 3.

If it is assumed, without loss of generality, that the number of new entrants in the interval $(0, dt)$ is dt, then the number of new entrants in the interval $(t, t + dt)$ would be $e^{\rho t} dt$. Similarly, if the general level of salaries at the outset of the scheme is taken as one monetary unit, the level of salaries at time t would be $e^{\gamma t}$. A unit pension would grow to $e^{\beta t}$ in t years.

1.3 THE ACTIVE POPULATION AND RETIRED POPULATION FUNCTIONS

For the theoretical development, time is regarded as a continuous variable with one year as the unit. The two key functions which describe the demographic development of a retirement pension scheme are:

- the active population function $A(t)$; and
- the retired population function $R(t)$.

Both are assumed to be continuous, differentiable functions.

Strictly speaking, these functions should be regarded as stochastic. The demographic projections established on the basis of the assumed parameters in fact represent average or expected values of $A(t)$ and $R(t)$. The actual values which would be realized are governed by the respective probability distributions and are therefore uncertain. The classical actuarial approach based on expected values – the so-called "deterministic" approach – will be followed in this book, but the underlying stochastic nature of the functions should be appreciated.

Consider a pension scheme which operates without any fundamental changes, such as a significant modification of the benefit provisions or an appreciable expansion of its scope of coverage, except for a steady flow of new entrants (at force of growth ρ). It is also assumed, as is generally the case, that persons already over retirement age at the outset of the scheme are not entitled to any benefit.

The following development assumes a fixed entry age for new entrants – say b – and a fixed retirement age – say r – but the same reasoning can be applied to any other combination of entry and retirement ages, so that the results established below are of more general validity.

A Lexis diagram (Bowers et al., 1986, p. 511; Daykin et al., 1994, p. 442) is useful to visualize the components of a pension scheme, as well as the process of its evolution (see figure 1 – page 107 – of Appendix 2). Time is shown along the horizontal axis and age along the vertical; the point (x, y) represents persons aged y at time x. The diagram relates to persons who enter the scheme at age b (=20) and retire at age r (=65), ω (=100) being the limit of life. Then each diagonal, such as ABE, represents a cohort of members and traces it from entry through retirement up to its eventual disappearance. Each vertical line, such as ET, represents persons living at the same time, either as active persons or as retired persons. Certain zones have particular significance; the triangle ABC represents the future lifetime which will be spent in active participation in the scheme by the initial population, while the parallelogram $BCDE$ depicts the future lifetime which will be spent as pensioners by the same group. The open-ended areas to the right of AB and BE represent the corresponding lifetimes of future entrants.

Assuming that those over the retirement age at the outset are excluded, the number of retirees in a new pension scheme will start from zero and increase steadily for several years as members keep retiring and deaths from among the retired do not offset the new additions to the pension roll. Eventually, when the entire initial population has disappeared, the rate of increase will reduce and settle down to a steady rate. This result can be demonstrated as follows for those entering at the fixed age b. In the Lexis diagram (figure 1), if $FJ = \sigma$ years, the number of pensioners at S would be $e^{\rho\sigma}$ times the number at R (under the assumption of the constancy, over time, of the rates of decrement), and this will also be the case for any other pair of points R' and S' on the same verticals. Thus when the retired population consists only of survivors of new entrants, it would grow at the instantaneous rate ρ; the same result would also apply to the active population. At that stage, the force of growth of the total insured population would become identical to the force of growth of new entrants.

The ratio of the number of pensioners to the active population – referred to as the aged dependency ratio – will, typically, display a similar growth trend; it will increase from zero, initially rather rapidly but then more slowly until it reaches a constant level. At that stage, say $t = \omega_1$, the scheme is said to have attained demographic maturity.

The characteristics of the functions $R(t)$ and $A(t)$ can be symbolically expressed as follows:

$$R'(t) > 0 \tag{1.1a}$$

$$\frac{R'(t)}{R(t)} > \frac{A'(t)}{A(t)} \qquad (t < \omega_1) \tag{1.1b}$$

$$\frac{R'(t)}{R(t)} = \frac{A'(t)}{A(t)} = \rho \qquad (t \geq \omega_1) \tag{1.1c}$$

1.4 THE EXPENDITURE AND INSURED SALARY FUNCTIONS

The two key functions which characterize the financial development of a pension scheme are:

- the expenditure function $B(t)$; and
- the insured salary function $S(t)$.

To begin with, $B(t)$ is regarded as relating to benefit expenditure only. Both functions are assumed to be continuous, differentiable functions. The total benefit expenditure and the total insured salary bill in the interval $(z, z + dz)$ will then be given by $B(z)\,dz$ and $S(z)\,dz$.

As in the case of the demographic functions $A(t)$ and $R(t)$, the functions $B(t)$ and $S(t)$ are also stochastic in nature and the projected values represent the expected values of these functions. To take into account the variability of these functions about their averages would require recourse to risk theory, which is yet to be widely applied in the area of pension financing (see section 3.12 of Chapter 3). The approach in this book is based on the classical "deterministic" approach, but the underlying stochastic nature of the functions should be borne in mind.

The term "replacement rate" refers to the percentage which the initial pension amount bears to the salary basis of the award, for example, the salary of the insured person at retirement. The "pension amount", at any subsequent time, refers to the monetary amount of the pension, taking into account indexation of the pension since its award.

A typical pattern of growth of $B(t)$ and $S(t)$ is described below. The trend of the expenditure function $B(t)$ will, in the first instance, depend on the trend of the retired population described in section 1.3, above. In addition, it will be influenced by the average amount of the pensions in payment. In this regard, an important distinction is between the case where the initially insured population receives special credits to compensate for the late start of the scheme – for example, full recognition of periods of past service – and that where no such credits are awarded.

In the latter case the replacement rate of new awardees will increase steadily until retirements begin to take place after a full insurance career; consequently, the average replacement rate of all current pensions will also increase, although at a steadily decreasing pace, until it reaches a constant level when all current pensioners are composed of persons who have retired after a full insurance career. In contrast, if the past service periods of the initial population are fully recognized, the replacement rate will be practically constant from the outset. Thus, the extent of past service credits will have a profound influence on the trend of $B(t)$ until the time when the initial population completely disappears.

In either case, $B(t)$ will increase, from zero at the outset, but the rate of increase will eventually slow down and reach a steady pace ($= \rho + \gamma$), being the force of growth of the retired population plus that of the average pension amount. That the average pension amount grows at force γ can be demonstrated with reference to the Lexis diagram (figure 1). Considering those entering at the fixed age b, the average pension amount at S would be $e^{\gamma\sigma}$ times that at R, reflecting the increase in the salary at retirement from G to K; this will also be the case for any other pair R', S' on the same verticals. Hence the overall average pension amount grows at the instantaneous rate γ.

Thus, while the absolute value of $B(t)$ will depend on the rate of pension indexation, β, the eventual growth trend of $B(t)$ is not affected by it. For although each individual pension amount grows at the rate β, the average amount of all current pensions grows at γ, due to what is known as the replacement effect; pensioners at every age are continuously replaced by others with correspondingly higher pension amounts, being based on a final salary growing with force γ.

The ratio $B(t)/S(t)$ will, typically, display a similar trend, growing from zero to eventually reach a constant level at the point in time, say $t = \omega_2$, when the scheme attains what may be termed financial maturity. It will be evident that demographic maturity will generally precede financial maturity and that the more generous the past service credits to the initial population, the earlier the attainment of financial maturity. This is illustrated in figure 2 (page 107), which is based on the hypothetical pension scheme developed in Appendix 2.

Apart from the characteristics of $B(t)$, as already described, the relationship between $B(t)$ and $S(t)$ is particularly important for the discussion of financial systems. Symbolically,

$$B'(t) > 0 \tag{1.2a}$$

$$\frac{B'(t)}{B(t)} > \frac{S'(t)}{S(t)} \qquad (t < \omega_2) \tag{1.2b}$$

$$\frac{B'(t)}{B(t)} = \frac{S'(t)}{S(t)} = \rho + \gamma \qquad (t \geq \omega_2) \tag{1.2c}$$

Up to this point the administration expenses of operating the scheme have not been mentioned. If the operating expenses are financed independently, for example met directly out of the government budget, they are clearly not relevant. Where this is not the case, these expenses will need to be considered.

In the initial stages of a new pension scheme administration expenditure may predominate, but as the scheme matures, its importance relative to the expenditure on benefits will fall considerably. Administrative expenditure, in the long run, can be regarded as roughly proportional to benefit expenditure or, alternatively, as approximately linearly related to both benefit expenditure and insured salaries. In either case, the total expenditure function will bear a relationship, similar to that of the benefit expenditure function, to the insured salary function. Thus, the characteristics indicated in (1.2) can be assumed to hold even if $B(t)$ is defined so as to include administration expenditure. This is assumed to be the case hereafter.

1.5 THE THEORETICAL BASIS OF FINANCIAL SYSTEMS

Social security schemes, which are sponsored by national governments, are assumed to be of infinite duration, that is, it is taken for granted that there will be a regular flow of new entrants indefinitely into the future. Because of this, financial systems for social security pension schemes are based on the so-called *open fund* approach, which considers the initial population and future entrants as a single group for this purpose. Any financial system essentially aims at achieving an equilibrium between income and outgo of the scheme – without necessarily equating contributions to current expenditure, which is only one way of achieving the equilibrium. In fact, an important consequence of the maturing process of a pension scheme, described in section 1.4 above, is that there are, in theory, an infinity of financial systems which may be applied to the scheme.

For the discussion of financial systems, two additional functions are now introduced:

- the contribution rate function $C(t)$, which characterizes the financial system; and
- the reserve function $V(t)$, which represents the excess of inflow over outflow, accumulated with interest at force δ.

These functions are connected to the functions $B(t)$ and $S(t)$ by the fundamental differential equation (Zelenka, 1958, p. 369):

$$dV(t) = V(t)\delta\, dt + C(t)S(t)\, dt - B(t)\, dt \tag{1.3}$$

In other words, the change in the reserve in any small interval is equal to the investment income on the reserve in the interval plus the excess of contribution income over benefit expenditure in the same interval.

By integrating the above equation over the interval (n, m), the following relationship is obtained between the values of the reserve function at $t = n$ and $t = m$:

$$V(m)\, e^{-\delta m} = V(n)\, e^{-\delta n} + \int_n^m [C(t)S(t) - B(t)]\, e^{-\delta t}\, dt \tag{1.4}$$

The expression for $V(m)$ is then obtained as

$$V(m) = V(n)\, e^{\delta(m-n)} + \int_n^m [C(t)S(t) - B(t)]\, e^{\delta(m-t)}\, dt \tag{1.5}$$

In particular, putting $n = 0$ and taking $V(0) = 0$, the following *retrospective* expression for $V(m)$ is obtained:

$$V(m) = e^{\delta m} \int_0^m [C(t)S(t) - B(t)]\, e^{-\delta t}\, dt \tag{1.6}$$

An equation of equilibrium can be written for the entire duration of a pension scheme. The equivalence of receipts and payments, taking into account the time value of money, can be expressed by equating, at the outset of the scheme, the present value of the future contribution stream to the present value of future expenditures:

$$\int_0^\infty C(t)S(t)\,e^{-\delta t}\,dt = \int_0^\infty B(t)\,e^{-\delta t}\,dt \tag{1.7}$$

assuming that the two integrals converge – which will be the case if (1.2) holds and $\delta > \rho + \gamma$. The above equation is the fundamental equation of equilibrium of a new pension scheme. It implies that

$$\int_0^m [C(t)S(t) - B(t)]\,e^{-\delta t}\,dt = \int_m^\infty [B(t) - C(t)S(t)]\,e^{-\delta t}\,dt \tag{1.8}$$

Substituting in expression (1.6), the following *prospective* expression is obtained for the reserve function:

$$V(m) = e^{\delta m} \int_m^\infty [B(t) - C(t)S(t)]\,e^{-\delta t}\,dt \tag{1.9}$$

If a view is taken, at the outset, of the entire lifetime of the scheme, any contribution function $C(t)$ which satisfies the fundamental equation of equilibrium (1.7) constitutes a theoretically possible financial system for a new pension scheme, and leads to the corresponding reserve function $V(m)$ given by (1.6) or (1.9). However, practical expediency makes it necessary to impose a condition on each of $C(t)$ and $V(t)$. Negative values of $C(t)$ – implying that the scheme is reimbursing the contributing parties – or negative values of $V(t)$ – implying that the scheme is borrowing to pay current benefits – will need to be excluded. Symbolically, it is necessary that $C(t) \geq 0$ and $V(t) \geq 0$ for all values of t. The imposition of these and other conditions on $C(t)$ and/or $V(t)$ leads to various specific financial systems.

1.6   THE PAY-AS-YOU-GO FINANCIAL SYSTEM

Theoretically, the pay-as-you-go (PAYG) financial system can be defined by the condition $V(t) = 0$ for all values of t. From the fundamental differential equation (1.3), it can then be deduced that

$$C(t) = \frac{B(t)}{S(t)} \tag{1.10}$$

With reference to the Lexis diagram (figure 1), it will be seen that the PAYG system achieves financial equilibrium along vertical lines such as ET, with the active persons bearing the cost of benefits to the pensioners living at the same time.

In practice the system cannot operate on a continuous basis; it will have to be defined with reference to a finite interval of time. If a year is taken as the interval, the system is termed the annual PAYG or annual assessment system. The condition on the reserve would then be that $V(t) = 0$ for integral values of t. In equation (1.4), putting $m = n + 1$ and $V(n) = V(n + 1) = 0$, the level contribution rate over the $(n + 1)$th year of operation of the scheme is given by

$$\text{PAYG}_{n+1} = \frac{\int_n^{n+1} B(t)\, e^{-\delta t}\, dt}{\int_n^{n+1} S(t)\, e^{-\delta t}\, dt} \tag{1.11}$$

If contribution inflow and benefit outflow are assumed to be uniformly distributed over the year, the contribution rate can be expressed as

$$\text{PAYG}_{n+1} = \frac{\int_n^{n+1} B(t)\, dt}{\int_n^{n+1} S(t)\, dt} \tag{1.12}$$

However, inflow of cash within the year may not exactly match outgo. Moreover, allowance will need to be made for unexpected variations from the projected values of the contribution income or the benefit expenditure over the year. It is therefore the practice to add a small margin to the calculated contribution rate in order to build up a *contingency reserve* to sustain cash flow.

1.7 THE GENERAL AVERAGE PREMIUM SYSTEM AND ITS DERIVATIVES

The general average premium (GAP) system is based on the concept of a constant contribution rate applicable throughout the subsequent lifetime of the pension scheme. Taking the view at $t = m$ and putting $C(t) = C$ (a constant) in (1.9), the following expression is obtained for the general average premium for the interval (m, ∞):

$$C = \frac{\int_m^\infty B(t)\, e^{-\delta t}\, dt - V(m)\, e^{-\delta m}}{\int_m^\infty S(t)\, e^{-\delta t}\, dt} \tag{1.13}$$

More particularly, if the view is taken at the outset of the scheme, the general average premium – indicated by GAP – will be given by

$$\text{GAP} = \frac{\int_0^\infty B(t)\, e^{-\delta t}\, dt}{\int_0^\infty S(t)\, e^{-\delta t}\, dt} \tag{1.14}$$

The subsequent discussion is based on the GAP defined by equation (1.14).

Let the functions $B(t)$ and $S(t)$ be partitioned as follows:

$$B(t) = B1(t) + B2(t); \qquad S(t) = S1(t) = S2(t)$$

where $B1(t)$ and $S1(t)$ relate to the initial population and $B2(t)$ and $S2(t)$ relate to future entrants.

An average premium AP1 for the initial population and an average premium AP2 for new entrants can be determined as follows:

$$\text{AP1} = \frac{\int_0^\infty B1(t)\,e^{-\delta t}\,dt}{\int_0^\infty S1(t)\,e^{-\delta t}\,dt} \tag{1.15}$$

$$\text{AP2} = \frac{\int_0^\infty B2(t)\,e^{-\delta t}\,dt}{\int_0^\infty S2(t)\,e^{-\delta t}\,dt} \tag{1.16}$$

The GAP can then be expressed as follows:

$$\text{GAP} = \frac{\text{AP1}\int_0^\infty S1(t)\,e^{-\delta t}\,dt + \text{AP2}\int_0^\infty S2(t)\,e^{-\delta t}\,dt}{\int_0^\infty S(t)\,e^{-\delta t}\,dt} \tag{1.17}$$

This shows that the GAP can be regarded as a weighted average of AP1 and AP2.

In the Lexis diagram (figure 1), AP1 is the average premium paid by the active lives in triangle *ABC* to support the benefits of the pensioners in the parallelogram *BCDE*, while AP2 is the average premium payable by those in the open-ended zone to the right of *AB* to support the cost of pensions to those in the open-ended zone to the right of *BE*. The GAP can be interpreted in a similar way.

The average premium for the initial population can generally be expected to be higher than that for new entrants, owing to the effect of past service credits. Even if no such credits are awarded, this will be the case unless the pension formula is scaled somewhat more than proportionately to the duration of contributory service, which would be unusual, especially in a social security pension scheme. The following inequality relationship will therefore hold:

$$\text{AP1} > \text{GAP} > \text{AP2} \tag{1.18}$$

To facilitate the discussion of "full funding" (see section 1.13, below) and to establish a link with financial systems for occupational pension schemes – to be discussed in Chapter 2 – it is instructive to consider a hypothetical financial system where the initial population pays its own average premium (AP1), while new entrants pay their average premium (AP2). This is equivalent to a system where the contribution rate function $C(t)$ is the weighted average of AP1 and AP2, the weights being the respective insured salary functions, at time t, of the initial population and the new entrants. For the purpose of identification this system will be called the "autonomous funding system" (AFS), although this is not standard terminology. The function $C(t)$ will start at AP1 and will gradually reduce to AP2 when the whole initial population has retired. The contribution rate under this system is therefore initially higher than the GAP, but eventually lower than the GAP. This means that a higher reserve will be generated than under the GAP.

1.8   THE TERMINAL FUNDING SYSTEM

Among the several intermediate financial systems, between the PAYG and GAP systems, the terminal funding system deserves special mention. This financial system is usually applied to pension benefits provided under employment injury insurance schemes. It has occasionally been applied to social security pensions. This system has sometimes been referred to as the "assessment of constituent capitals" system, in other words, full pre-funding at the time of award.

Let $Ka(t)\,dt$ represent the capitalized value of the pensions awarded in the interval $(t, t + dt)$. Then the present value of future benefit expenditures can also be expressed in terms of the function $Ka(t)$, as follows:

$$\int_0^\infty B(t)\,e^{-\delta t}\,dt = \int_0^\infty Ka(t)\,e^{-\delta t}\,dt \tag{1.19}$$

This can be explained by reference to the Lexis diagram (figure 1). Thus, pensions paid along the line BE are discounted in two steps; first to the point B and then to the point C. The left and right hand sides of equation (1.19) are thus two different ways of discounting future pension expenditures.

The fundamental equation of equilibrium (1.7) can therefore be expressed as

$$\int_0^\infty C(t)S(t)\,e^{-\delta t}\,dt = \int_0^\infty Ka(t)\,e^{-\delta t}\,dt \tag{1.20}$$

An obvious solution to the above equation, denoted by TFS(t), is

$$\text{TFS}(t) = \frac{Ka(t)}{S(t)} \tag{1.21}$$

This yields the financial system of terminal funding, so called because each pension is capitalized at the time it is awarded. With reference again to the Lexis diagram (figure 1), it will be seen that the terminal funding system achieves equilibrium over lines such as ACD, the active lives on AC bearing the cost of benefits to the pensioners on CD.

If the initial population does not receive past service credits, $Ka(t)$ will increase steeply, from zero at the outset, up to the attainment of demographic maturity, after which it will settle down to the steady growth rate of $\rho + \gamma$. TFS(t) will exhibit a similar trend, reaching a constant level at the onset of demographic maturity. If the initial population benefits from past service credits, the initial growth trend will be moderated. If past service is fully credited, TFS(t) may not vary appreciably with t, and the system will therefore tend to the GAP system.

The reserve $V(n)$, representing the capitalized value of current pensions, is given by

$$V(n) = e^{\delta n} \int_0^n [Ka(t) - B(t)]\,e^{-\delta t}\,dt \tag{1.22}$$

In practice, the terminal funding system will not operate on a continuous basis, but will be applied over finite time intervals (for example, annual periods). It is hereafter denoted by the acronym TFS.

1.9   SYSTEMS BASED ON SUCCESSIVE CONTROL PERIODS

A whole series of intermediate financial systems, between the PAYG and GAP systems, can be generated by dividing the time span of a pension scheme into successive intervals of limited duration and determining a level contribution rate for each interval such that the reserve function $V(t)$ satisfies a given condition over the interval. For example, the period up to financial maturity $(0, \omega_2)$ may be divided into h intervals – not necessarily equal – followed by a final interval (ω_2, ∞).

Let (n, m) denote any one of these intervals. Equation (1.4) can be regarded as the equation of equilibrium for this interval. Moreover, the expression for the reserve function at any intermediate time point u $(n \leq u \leq m)$ – following (1.5) – will be

$$V(u) = V(n)\, e^{\delta(u-n)} + \int_n^u [C(t)S(t) - B(t)]\, e^{\delta(u-t)}\, dt \qquad (1.23)$$

Subject to the basic conditions $C(t) \geq 0$ and $V(t) \geq 0$, other conditions could be imposed on $C(t)$ or $V(u)$. For example, if $V(n) = V(m) = 0$, the financial system is that of assessment over several years at a time rather than yearly, as in the annual PAYG system. A reserve would build up during each interval but would reduce to zero at the end of the interval. The level contribution rate (denoted by C) for the interval will then be given by

$$C = \frac{\int_n^m B(t)\, e^{-\delta t}\, dt}{\int_n^m S(t)\, e^{-\delta t}\, dt} \qquad (1.24)$$

Another variant specifies the "reserve ratio" at $t = m$ (Hirose, 1996). This ratio is defined as

$$\kappa = \frac{V(t)}{B(t)} \qquad (1.25)$$

If the required value of the reserve ratio is κ_0, substituting for $V(m)$ in (1.4) and simplifying, the following expression is obtained for the level contribution rate:

$$C = \frac{\kappa_0 B(m)\, e^{-\delta m} + \int_n^m B(t)\, e^{-\delta t}\, dt - V(n)\, e^{-\delta n}}{\int_n^m S(t)\, e^{-\delta t}\, dt} \qquad (1.26)$$

More stringently, a minimum reserve ratio κ_0 might be required throughout the interval (n, m). In this case, the level contribution rate is the maximum of those resulting from the application of the above formula for each sub-interval (n, u), $n < u < m$ – in practice, for integral values of u.

A further variant specifies the "balance ratio" at $t = m$ (*ibid.*). This ratio is defined as

$$\lambda = \frac{B(t) - CS(t)}{\delta V(t)} \tag{1.27}$$

This ratio indicates the extent to which the interest on the reserve, or the reserve itself, is used, on top of current contributions, for balancing current expenditure. If $\lambda < 0$, even the interest income is not required for this purpose; if $0 < \lambda < 1$, a part of the interest income is used; and if $\lambda > 1$, in addition to the interest, recourse is had to the reserve itself. If the required balance ratio at $t = m$ is λ_0, substitution in (1.4) yields, after simplification,

$$C = \frac{B(m) e^{-\delta m} + \delta\lambda_0 \int_n^m B(t) e^{-\delta t} dt - \delta\lambda_0 V(n) e^{-\delta n}}{S(m) e^{-\delta m} + \delta\lambda_0 \int_n^m S(t) e^{-\delta t} dt} \tag{1.28}$$

Again, more stringently, λ_0 might be specified as a maximum for the balance ratio for the whole interval (n,m). The level contribution rate will then be the maximum of those resulting from the application of the above formula for each sub-interval (n, u), $n < u < m$.

The case where $\lambda = 1$ at $t = m$ (with $\lambda < 1$ for $n < t < m$) is of particular interest. This signifies that the reserve grows throughout the interval (n, m) and attains a local maximum at $t = m$. This corresponds to the so-called "scaled premium" system, which was designed by ILO actuaries and widely applied, particularly in developing countries. This is treated in detail in section 1.10, below.

A general formula connecting the level contribution rate in the final interval (ω_2, ∞), denoted by π, with the expenditure, salary and reserve functions at $t = \omega_2$ can be derived as follows:

The equation of equilibrium at $t = \omega_2$ can be written as

$$V(\omega_2) + \pi \int_0^\infty S(\omega_2 + z) e^{-\delta z} dz = \int_0^\infty B(\omega_2 + z) e^{-\delta z} dz \tag{1.29}$$

But $S(\omega_2 + z) = S(\omega_2) e^{(\rho+\gamma)z}$, with a similar expression for $B(\omega_2 + z)$, due to the status of financial maturity beyond $t = \omega_2$.

Substituting and simplifying, the following result is obtained, subject to $\delta > \rho + \gamma$:

$$V(\omega_2)(\delta - \rho - \gamma) = B(\omega_2) - \pi S(\omega_2) \tag{1.30}$$

1.10 THE SCALED PREMIUM SYSTEM

The scaled premium system can be regarded as a particular case of the systems based on successive control periods. However, this system is treated independently in this section.

In its original formulation (Zelenka, 1958) this system was conceived as follows: a level contribution rate which would balance income and expenditure over a limited initial period of years $(0, n_1)$ – called the first period of equilibrium – is determined, but is actually applied over a shorter period $(0, n_1')$ during which the reserve grows continuously and reaches a local maximum at $t = n_1'$. A higher, level contribution rate is then determined for a second period of equilibrium (n_1', n_2), under the condition $V(n_2) = V(n_1')$, but is applied over a shorter period (n_1', n_2') during which the reserve grows and reaches another local maximum at $t = n_2'$, and so on.

The term "scaled premium system" has been defined more generally, to indicate one characterized by steadily increasing level contribution rates in successive control periods and a non-decreasing reserve fund (Thullen, 1973, p.V-27). The specific variant, under which the reserve attains a local maximum at the end of each period, has been developed mathematically (Thullen, 1964), enabling the direct choice of the intervals $(0, n_1'), (n_1', n_2')$, and so on, and the determination of the respective level contribution rates. This variant is discussed below.

Consider any one of the intervals (n, m). Let $\pi(n, m)$ represent the level contribution rate in this interval. Assuming that the reserve reaches a local maximum at $t = m$, $V'(m) = 0$. Substituting in the fundamental differential equation (1.3), the following expression for the terminal reserve is obtained:

$$V(m) = \frac{B(m) - \pi(n, m)S(m)}{\delta} \tag{1.31}$$

Substituting for $V(m)$ in the general expression for the reserve (1.4) and simplifying, the following expression is obtained for the level premium for the interval (n, m):

$$\pi(n, m) = \frac{B(m)\,e^{-\delta m} + \delta \int_n^m B(z)\,e^{-\delta z}\,dz - \delta V(n)\,e^{-\delta n}}{S(m)\,e^{-\delta m} + \delta \int_n^m S(z)\,e^{-\delta z}\,dz} \tag{1.32}$$

It can be shown that the conditions $B'(t) > 0$ and that $B(t)/S(t)$ is a non-decreasing function are sufficient to ensure a positive non-decreasing reserve in (n, m), as required. In addition, under these conditions, the level premium calculated according to formula (1.32) will be positive and exceed the level premium calculated according to the same formula in the preceding interval (see Appendix 5).

Suppose the infinite time span of the pension scheme is divided into $h + 1$ intervals, the last corresponding to the period of financial maturity (ω_2, ∞). Starting from $V(0) = 0$, the repeated application of the above formulae alternately will yield the scaled premium contribution rates $\pi(1) \ldots \pi(h)$ for each of the first h intervals and the corresponding terminal reserves. $\pi(h + 1)$ can then be expressed in terms of $\pi(h)$ and the ultimate PAYG contribution rate as follows:

Applying the formula (1.31) to the hth interval,

$$V(\omega_2)\delta = B(\omega_2) - \pi(h)S(\omega_2)$$

On the other hand, because of (1.30),

$$V(\omega_2)(\delta - \rho - \gamma) = B(\omega_2) - \pi(h + 1)S(\omega_2)$$

Eliminating $V(\omega_2)$, the following expression is obtained for $\pi(h+1)$:

$$\pi(h+1) = \pi(h)\left[1 - \frac{\rho+\gamma}{\delta}\right] + \left[\frac{\rho+\gamma}{\delta}\right]\text{PAYG}^* \qquad (1.33)$$

where PAYG* denotes the pay-as-you-go premium in the financially mature situation.

To complete this section, mention is made of another variant of the scaled premium system, where the condition on the terminal reserve is changed as follows: the force of growth of the reserve at the end of each interval is equal to the force of growth in the financially mature situation, i.e.

$$V'(t) = (\rho+\gamma)V(t) \text{ at the end of each interval.}$$

In this case also the expressions for the contribution rates and reserves – (1.31) and (1.32) – are valid except that δ should be replaced by $\delta - \rho - \gamma$ wherever it occurs. Additionally, $\pi(h+1) = \pi(h)$. The two variants of the scaled premium system are hereafter identified by the acronyms SCP1 and SCP2.

1.11 ASSESSMENT AND COMPARISON OF THE FINANCIAL SYSTEMS

The problem of financing a social security pension scheme can be regarded as essentially that of fixing the initial and future contribution rates at levels considered affordable by the respective contributing parties while, at the same time, tailoring the accumulation of the reserve to the projected investment needs and absorptive capacity of the economy. Further, for legislative or administrative convenience, the revision of the contribution rate should not be too frequent. The various systems are assessed below from this perspective.

From the point of view of the funding level, the PAYG system is at the lower extremity of the range of the practicable financial systems for a pension scheme. It involves an almost continuous increase in the contribution rate. Moreover, the contribution rate will reach a relatively very high level when the scheme attains financial maturity. Finally, practically no reserve will accumulate.

The GAP system has the advantage of a perpetually level contribution rate, but this means that a relatively high rate will need to be applied right at the outset. From the point of funding level, it is customary to regard the GAP system as the upper extreme of financial systems applicable to social security pension schemes. Thus the system will lead to the accumulation of a substantial reserve.

The terminal funding system (TFS) has the property that the reserve is adequate to cover the future cost of all pensions already awarded, although this may not be a requirement for social security pension financing.

The system of successive control periods provides a balance between the contrary characteristics of the PAYG and the GAP systems. Thus the contribution rate can be maintained level for limited periods of time, so that the revision of the contribution rate is required only at intervals. Moreover, the accumulation of the reserve would be moderate. Considerable flexibility is available in the choice of the intervals and in controlling the levels of the contribution rates, as well as of the reserve accumulation.

The scaled premium system provides for a non-decreasing reserve, so that in theory recourse is had only to the investment income on the reserve, but not the reserve itself. It would therefore be possible to invest the reserve in assets which need never be liquidated.

1.12   ILLUSTRATION OF THE FINANCIAL SYSTEMS

Figures 3 to 8 of Appendix 2 (pages 108 to 110) illustrate the contribution rates and reserves for the various financing systems discussed above. The reserve is shown as a multiple of the insured salary bill rather than in monetary terms, to facilitate inter-system comparisons. The PAYG and GAP systems, which are convenient reference points, are included in all the figures. Figures 3 to 6 illustrate the TFS and the "autonomous funding system" (AFS), including the sensitivity of these systems to past service credits. Figures 7 and 8 relate to the two variants of the scaled premium system. These figures are based on the hypothetical pension scheme developed in Appendix 2.

The first comparison that can be made is between the different financial systems, for a given level of past service credits. As regards contribution rates, it is seen that as a rule, the lower the initial rates, the higher the ultimate rates and vice versa. Under all systems – except the AFS – the initial contribution rates are below the GAP level, but ultimately above the GAP level. Under PAYG the initial rates are the lowest, but the ultimate rates are the highest. The TFS and the scaled premium system (SCP) are intermediate between PAYG and GAP, at different levels. The AFS is the exception, with the initial rates higher than, but the ultimate rates lower than, the GAP.

As regards the accumulation of the reserve, the lower the ultimate contribution rate, the higher the level of the reserve. Thus, the AFS produces the highest ultimate accumulation, followed by the GAP. The other systems produce lower ultimate reserves, in inverse order to their respective ultimate contribution rates.

The effect of past service credits is particularly significant with regard to the relative levels of the AFS, GAP and TFS. The AFS approaches the GAP system when there are no credits but diverges from it substantially if past service is fully credited. In contrast, the TFS approaches the GAP under full past service crediting – in this illustrative example the two systems are identical – but diverges significantly from it when past service is not credited.

These differential trends of contribution rates and reserves imply different levels of inter-generational transfer, within the framework of the pension scheme per se. The PAYG system has the highest level of such transfer. The AFS can be regarded as the system with zero transfer from new entrants to the initial population. All other systems involve some measure of inter-generational transfer, including the GAP system. It will also be noted that, for any given system, the more generous the past service credits, the larger the extent of inter-generational transfer.

An instructive comparison is between the reserve of any given system and the reserve of the TFS. As seen before, the TFS reserve equals the capitalized value of all current pensions. When the system reserve exceeds the TFS reserve, the balance represents the reserve for active persons, that is, it is a security for the accruing benefit rights of those who are not yet retired. Although this point is more relevant to occupational pension schemes than to social security pension schemes, it may be noted that several of the financial systems applied in social security may not carry a sufficient reserve even to cover the capital value of current pensions. The GAP system reserve generally provides some cover in respect of active persons, although this may be insignificant when full past service credits are awarded to initial entrants.

1.13 THE CONCEPT OF FULL FUNDING IN RELATION TO THE GAP SYSTEM

The term "full funding" is increasingly being used in the context of pension financing. However, it is important to note that the GAP system, which is at the upper end of the range of financial systems applied in the area of social security pension financing, is in general not fully funded.

A pension scheme is said to be fully funded if the accumulated reserve at least equals the value of all accrued benefits, which includes, in addition to the capital value of current pensions, the value of benefits earned to date by active members (Tilove, 1976, pp. 149, 152). In other words, should the scheme be wound up, the reserve on hand, together with future interest earnings, would suffice to pay all current pensions until their extinction and also to pay all accrued pensions of active members, whenever due under the rules of the scheme and for the specified durations. It should, however, be noted that when a pension scheme is described as being "on full funding", it does not mean that it has achieved a fully funded position; it means that it is on a schedule intended to achieve that goal (ibid., p. 152).

There are, of course, some technical difficulties in defining accrued pensions; for example, whether anticipated future increase in the insured salary should be taken into account and whether indexation of pensions after award should be allowed for. This problem apart, the question which arises is whether, on some definition of accrued benefits, the GAP system is a full funding system.

To answer this question, it is recalled that when past service is fully credited, the GAP system approaches the TFS, with the result that the reserve is practically equal to the capital value of current pensions. This means that the reserve available for active members will be unlikely to cover the value of their accrued benefits on any definition, so that the GAP system will not lead to a fully funded position. However, it was seen that when there are no past service credits, the GAP system approaches the AFS. The discussion in Chapter 2 will show that the AFS does lead to a fully funded position when the initially insured population has fully retired.

Thus, generally speaking, the GAP system cannot be characterized as a full funding system, although it may approximate to such a system, for example, when no past service credits are given to the initial population. Therefore, the label "partially funded" will apply practically without exception to all financial systems employed in the area of social security pension financing.

THE FUNDING OF OCCUPATIONAL PENSIONS

2

2.1 INTRODUCTION

This chapter is concerned with occupational pension schemes covering private sector employees, which are sponsored by individual employers or set up through negotiations by trade unions with several employers (multi-employer plans). The principles discussed are also applicable to public sector schemes which are funded. The subject will not be treated in detail; the purpose is only to indicate the principal differences between occupational and social security pension schemes in the approach to financing. As in Chapter 1, the discussion will be limited to retirement pensions based on a formula which is strictly proportional to the period of contributory service – specifically, accruing at 1 per cent per year – and to the terminal salary (at retirement) of the member.

The basic characteristics of occupational pension schemes – at least as far as retirement benefits are concerned – are not very different from those of social security pension schemes, and the discussion in sections 1.3 and 1.4 can be taken as being equally valid. There are, however, a series of special considerations which lead, in practice, to the adoption of financial systems which are different from those employed in the area of social security pensions.

It is assumed that the assets of the occupational scheme are separated from the assets of the sponsor and held in trust on behalf of the members. This is normally considered desirable in order to secure the pension benefits independently of the financial health of the sponsor. However, an exception is the "book reserve" system practised, for example, in Germany, whereby pension reserves are maintained in the sponsor's balance sheet, so that the pension assets are, in effect, invested in the sponsor's business; security for the pensions is provided through insolvency insurance which the sponsor is required to take out with a mutual insurer, supported by all employers running such book reserved schemes.

For similar reasons, the PAYG system is generally not considered a feasible method of financing an occupational pension scheme. There is the risk that the sponsor (the employer) may become insolvent or simply close down the business, in which case all pension rights (both existing and prospective) would be lost. Moreover, the employer – who would presumably be the major contributor to the scheme – is also likely to find it inconvenient, from the budgeting point of view, to arrange for outlays which increase continuously over time.

Here again, an exception is provided by the complementary pension schemes in France based on the *répartition par points* system, which is effectively PAYG. However, it should be noted that these schemes are nationwide and compulsory in coverage so that the risk is shared across employers and, moreover, are at an advanced state of maturity.

It will be appreciated that the above-mentioned objections to the application of the unfunded PAYG system to occupational pensions could also be raised against the various partial funding systems discussed in Chapter 1 because, in the event of discontinuance of the scheme, the reserve fund available may only partly cover the accrued pension rights and further – except for the GAP system – the contribution rate will generally have an increasing trend over time. Moreover, these systems involve inter-generational transfers, which are acceptable in a social security scheme but are not intended in an occupational scheme. Even if this concept does not apply to the employer's contributions, the accrual accounting principle suggests that the cost of an employee's pension should be charged over the period of his or her employment.

For these reasons, unlike a social security scheme, an occupational pension scheme generally aims to achieve financial equilibrium on a "closed fund" basis, meaning that only the existing membership is brought into the equation, excluding future entrants. In this manner, equilibrium is established independently of the recruitment of new entrants. However, provided future entrants are also, as a group, in financial equilibrium, the scheme will also be in actuarial balance on an "open fund" basis.

In this chapter, the terms "contributions" and "contribution rate" refer to the total financial resources allocated to the scheme, without differentiating between the employer's and the employee's shares. In practice, the employee's contribution rate is often fixed in the regulations, the employer paying the balance of the required total contributions.

When the PAYG system is excluded, it is customary to use the word "funding" instead of "financing", and this terminology is adopted in this chapter. Funding methods are also referred to as actuarial cost methods. There is a wide variety of actuarial cost methods and the principal methods are briefly surveyed below. It must be borne in mind, however, that the choice of method in any particular case will be conditioned by the regulatory provisions in force. These provisions will generally proscribe underfunding, to ensure the security of the pension expectations of the covered employees. On the other hand, since pension fund contributions are normally tax exempt, the regulations are also likely to disallow or discourage overfunding.

The actuarial cost methods can be divided into two groups: individual methods and aggregate methods. In individual methods the total results are obtained by summing the results for individuals; in aggregate methods they are determined on a collective basis. The methods can be further divided into accrued benefit methods and entry age methods (Trowbridge and Farr, 1976, p. 35; Bowers et al., 1986, pp. 544, 546). Individual methods are discussed in sections 2.2 to 2.7 below, and aggregate methods are considered in section 2.8.

2.2   INDIVIDUAL COST METHODS

Individual cost methods first address the financial equilibrium of new entrants and then consider the adjustments required to achieve the closed-fund equilibrium of the initial population. Taking retirement pensions as an example, the contributions paid over a new entrant generation's active lifetime should, by retirement age, accumulate to the capital value of the pensions of those attaining that age. In the Lexis diagram (figure 1) equilibrium would be achieved along lines such as ABE, the pensions of those on BE being financed by those on AB.

For simplicity, all new entrants are assumed to enter at a single age b and to retire at a single age r. Let $K(x)$ represent the age-related contribution rate function and $F(x)$ the reserve function per unit salary bill at entry ($b \leq x \leq r$). Both functions are assumed to be continuous and differentiable. The equation of equilibrium at entry, per unit salary bill, can be written as

$$\int_b^r \frac{l_z^a}{l_b^a} \frac{s_z}{s_b} K(z) \, e^{\gamma(z-b)} \, e^{-\delta(z-b)} \, dz = \frac{r-b}{100} \frac{l_r^a}{l_b^a} \frac{s_r}{s_b} e^{\gamma(r-b)} \, e^{-\delta(r-b)} \bar{a}_r \qquad (2.1)$$

where l_x^a represents the service table function and s_x the relative salary scale function, both assumed continuous and differentiable, and $\bar{a}_r$ is a continuous life annuity payable to retirees, based on force of interest $\delta - \beta$. The parameters δ, γ and β were defined in section 1.2 of Chapter 1.

The above equation can be simplified and expressed in terms of commutation functions as follows (see Appendix 1 and equation (6.4)):

$$\int_b^r D_z^{as(\delta-\gamma)} K(z) \, dz = \frac{r-b}{100} D_r^{as(\delta-\gamma)} \bar{a}_r^{p(\delta-\beta)} \qquad (2.2)$$

where the superscripts a and p respectively denote functions relating to active persons and retirees, the superscript s denotes that the salary scale function s_x is incorporated and the superscript in parentheses specifies the underlying force of interest.

Assuming that the experience coincides with the initial assumptions, the reserve function at age x per unit salary bill at entry can be derived by accumulating the contributions paid from age b to age x, as follows:

$$F(x) = \int_b^x \frac{l_z^a}{l_b^a} \frac{s_z}{s_b} K(z) \, e^{\gamma(z-b)} \, e^{\delta(x-z)} \, dz \qquad (2.3)$$

and then simplified and expressed in terms of commutation functions as follows:

$$F(x) = e^{\delta(x-b)} \int_b^x \frac{D_z^{as(\delta-\gamma)}}{D_b^{as(\delta-\gamma)}} K(z) \, dz \qquad (2.4)$$

Multiplying both sides by $e^{-\delta(x-b)}$ and then differentiating both sides with respect to x,

$$[F'(x) - \delta F(x)] e^{-\delta(x-b)} = \frac{D_x^{as(\delta-\gamma)}}{D_b^{as(\delta-\gamma)}} K(x) \qquad (2.5)$$

This gives the following expression for $K(x)$:

$$K(x) = \frac{D_b^{as(\delta-\gamma)}}{D_x^{as(\delta-\gamma)}} [F'(x) - \delta F(x)] e^{-\delta(x-b)} \qquad (2.6)$$

2.3   ACCRUED BENEFIT COST METHODS

Accrued benefit cost methods (also known as unit credit funding methods) fund in each time interval the portion of the ultimate pension benefit earned in that interval. Assuming that the experience coincides with the initial assumptions, this will automatically lead to the reserve fund $F(x)$ equal to the probable present value of the portion of the ultimate benefit accrued up to that age. Of the several possible variants, the following two are selected for illustration:

(a)   the accrued pension is based on current service and current salary, with allowance for indexation after award: this is referred to as ACC1 in the following discussion;

(b)   the accrued pension is based on current service and the projected salary at retirement, with allowance for indexation after award: this is referred to as ACC2.

Accrued benefit cost method ACC1

The probable present value at age x of the portion of the retirement pension accrued up to that age, per unit salary bill at entry, is given by

$$F(x) = \frac{x-b}{100} \frac{l_x^a}{l_b^a} \frac{s_x}{s_b} e^{\gamma(x-b)} e^{-\delta(r-x)} \frac{l_r^a}{l_x^a} \bar{a}_r^{p(\delta-\beta)} \qquad (2.7)$$

which, after simplification, yields, in terms of commutation functions,

$$F(x) = \frac{x-b}{100} [e^{(\gamma+\delta)(x-b)}] \frac{s_x}{s_b} \frac{D_r^{a(\delta)}}{D_b^{a(\delta)}} \bar{a}_r^{p(\delta-\beta)} \qquad (2.8)$$

Multiplying both sides by $e^{-\delta(x-b)}$, differentiating both sides with respect to x and substituting in (2.6) yields the following expression for $K(x)$:

$$K(x) = \frac{1}{100} \frac{D_r^{a(\delta)}}{D_x^{a(\delta)}} \left[1 + (x-b)\left(\frac{s_x'}{s_x} + \gamma\right)\right] \bar{a}_r^{p(\delta-\beta)} \tag{2.9}$$

The above expression can be interpreted by considering the contribution amount $K(x)\,dx$ in the interval $(x, x+dx)$ per unit of current salary. The part within the square brackets *times dx* would represent the increase in the pension rate (as a percentage of the current salary) in the interval, which has two components: the pension rate percentage already accrued – $(x-b)$ – increased in the proportion $(s_x'/s_x + \gamma)\,dx$ due to the combined effect of the salary scale and salary escalation; and the dx percentage earned due to the service in the interval itself.

Accrued benefit cost method ACC2

The only difference from ACC1 is that in expression (2.7), $s_x\,e^{\gamma(x-b)}$ should be replaced by $s_r\,e^{\gamma(r-b)}$. After simplification, the following expression is obtained for $F(x)$ in the case of ACC2:

$$F(x) = \frac{x-b}{100}\left[e^{\delta(x-b)}\right]\frac{D_r^{as(\delta-\gamma)}}{D_b^{as(\delta-\gamma)}}\bar{a}_r^{p(\delta-\beta)} \tag{2.10}$$

Differentiation with respect to x and substitution in (2.6) gives, after simplification,

$$K(x) = \frac{1}{100}\frac{D_r^{as(\delta-\gamma)}}{D_x^{as(\delta-\gamma)}}\bar{a}_r^{p(\delta-\beta)} \tag{2.11}$$

2.4 ENTRY AGE COST METHODS

Entry age methods (also called projected benefit methods) seek to establish a level contribution rate or amount in function of the entry age. In this case $K(x) = K(b)$ at all values of x. From the equation of equilibrium – (2.2) above – the following expression is obtained:

$$K(b) = \frac{r-b}{100}\frac{D_r^{as(\delta-\gamma)}}{\int_b^r D_z^{as(\delta-\gamma)}\,dz}\bar{a}_r^{p(\delta-\beta)} \tag{2.12}$$

which can be expressed as

$$K(b) = \frac{r-b}{100}\frac{D_r^{as(\delta-\gamma)}}{\bar{N}_b^{as(\delta-\gamma)}}\bar{a}_r^{p(\delta-\beta)} \tag{2.13}$$

where

$$\bar{N}_x^{as(\delta-\gamma)} = \int_x^r D_z^{as(\delta-\gamma)}\,dz$$

Assuming that the experience coincides with the initial assumptions, the reserve fund function will then be given by

$$F(x) = e^{\delta(x-b)} K(b) \frac{\int_b^x D_z^{as(\delta-\gamma)} \, dz}{D_b^{as(\delta-\gamma)}} \tag{2.14}$$

which can be expressed as

$$F(x) = e^{\delta(x-b)} K(b) \frac{\bar{N}_b^{as(\delta-\gamma)} - \bar{N}_x^{as(\delta-\gamma)}}{D_b^{as(\delta-\gamma)}} \tag{2.15}$$

This actuarial cost method will be referred to by the acronym ENT. If all cohorts enter at the same age b, $K(b)$ will be the average premium for all new entrants, that is, the premium AP2 discussed in section 1.7 of Chapter 1.

Figures 9 and 10 (page 111), based on the hypothetical pension scheme developed in Appendix 2, illustrate the working of the three actuarial cost methods over the contributory lifetime of a cohort entering at age 20 and retiring at age 65. The graphs of the $K(x)$ function in figure 9 show that the three methods fund the retirement benefit of the cohort at different paces. Figure 10 illustrates the build-up of the reserve fund to the capital value of the retirement pension over the contributory lifetime of the cohort; the steepness of the curve is in the (descending) order ENT, ACC2, ACC1, reflecting the relative paces of funding.

2.5 THE INITIAL ACCRUED LIABILITY AND ITS DISCHARGE

After dealing with the problem of the financial equilibrium of new entrants, the individual actuarial cost methods consider the adjustments required in order to achieve the closed fund financial equilibrium of the initial population.

The "normal cost", as a function of time, refers to the total contributions then payable by the active members based on the age-related contribution rate function $K(x)$. These contributions, however, will not suffice to produce an equilibrium for the initial population if full past service credits are awarded. The initial actuarial deficit arising on this account is termed the "initial accrued liability". It can be regarded as the cost of the scheme which will not be covered by future "normal cost" contributions, or – if past service is fully credited – as the fund which would be on hand had the actuarial cost method always been in application (Trowbridge and Farr, 1976, pp. 23–26).

The usual practice is for the sponsor to discharge the initial accrued liability through special payments, on top of the "normal cost" contributions to the scheme. Typically, level payments will be spread over a period of years, as generally required by legislation, ending in any case before the entire initial population has retired.

Alternatively this liability may be amortized, over the active lifetime of the initial insured population, by a fixed percentage of the salary bill, either of the total insured population or of the initial population alone. An extreme method of amortizing the initial accrued liability would be to pay only the interest on this liability, without ever repaying the capital. It will be noted that when the above-mentioned amortization plans are combined with the ENT system, the resulting systems will correspond, respectively, to the AFS and GAP systems discussed in Chapter 1.

In the extreme case, where no past service credits are awarded to the initial population, the initial accrued liability – defined, in this case, as the cost of pensions to be earned in virtue of future service, which will not be covered by future normal contributions – may well be negative at certain ages of the initial population, depending on the age-wise pace of funding of the specific actuarial cost method (see figure 9). Depending possibly also on the age distribution of the initial population, this could lead to an overall negative initial accrued liability. However, when partial past service credits are awarded leading to an overall positive initial accrued liability, it can be dealt with in the same manner as described above.

2.6 COMPARISON OF INDIVIDUAL COST METHODS WITH SOCIAL SECURITY FINANCING METHODS

In order to compare the above actuarial cost methods with the financing methods of social security pensions, it is necessary to characterize each method by a contribution rate function $C(t)$ and a reserve function $V(t)$ depending on time (t). The time-related contribution rate function would include two components:

(a) the "normal cost" contribution rate, which would be a weighted average of the age-related contribution rate function $K(x)$, based on the distribution of insured salaries by age at time t; and

(b) the additional contribution rate to amortize the initial accrued liability, that is, the instalment due at time t expressed as a percentage of the corresponding total salary bill.

As in Chapter 1, for the purpose of the demonstration it is assumed that the projection made at the outset of the scheme is realized exactly. Thus, any subsequent adjustments for actuarial gains and losses are ignored, although in practice there will be departures from projected results and adjustments will certainly be required.

The time-related contribution rate function would obviously be affected by the demographic and economic characteristics of the initial population. Figures 11 and 12 (page 112) relate to the hypothetical pension scheme developed in Appendix 2. Initial entrants are assumed to receive full credit in respect of pre-scheme service. Since the purpose is to illustrate the funding systems and to compare them with the social security financing systems, the actuarial basis and assumptions are identical to those used for the demonstration of the social security financing methods in Chapter 1, although in practice the basis for an occupational pension scheme may differ from that for a social security pension scheme – for example, the basis may incorporate a withdrawal decrement which is normally absent in the actuarial basis for a social security pension scheme.

In addition to the accrued benefit (ACC1, ACC2) and entry age (ENT) methods, the GAP system is included to serve as a reference point. The demonstrated ACC1, ACC2 and ENT cost methods discharge the initial accrued liability by level payments spread over the active lifetime of the youngest initial entrant.

It will be seen that the time-related contribution rates are initially well above the GAP, in the order ENT, ACC2, ACC1, while eventually they settle down to a level well below the GAP, in reverse order. A discontinuity occurs in the contribution rate function when the amortization of the initial accrued liability ceases.

As a consequence of the trends in the time-related contribution rates, the accumulated reserves of the actuarial cost methods are substantially higher than the GAP level, in reverse order to the ultimate levels of the contribution rates.

2.7   ASSESSMENT OF THE INDIVIDUAL ACTUARIAL COST METHODS

Any particular actuarial cost method could be judged on certain criteria (Lee, 1986, pp. 156–160) including, in particular:

- stability: how resilient is the "normal cost" contribution rate to changes in the age distribution of the active population?
- durability: how resilient is the "normal cost" contribution rate to a closure of the scheme to new entrants?
- security: how favourably does the time-related reserve fund compare with the accrued benefits of the members?

From figure 9 of Appendix 2, it can be inferred that if the age distribution of the active population shifted upwards, the "normal cost" contribution rate would be unaffected in the ENT method and slightly affected in the ACC2 method, but considerably affected (increased) in the ACC1 method. In the event of closure of the scheme to new entrants, the effect on ACC1 and ACC2 will be similar but more intense, while in the ENT system the "normal cost" contribution rate will again be unaffected. Thus the "stability" and "durability" ranking of the methods is ENT, ACC2, ACC1, in descending order.

As regards the aspect of "security", because of the way in which they are designed, the accrued benefit cost methods will automatically produce, in respect of new entrants, reserves which cover the "accrued benefits" on the specific definition. It should be recalled, however, that the ACC1 definition of accrued benefits is comparatively less generous and this method may, in certain circumstances, be regarded as not providing adequate security. As regards the entry age methods, figure 10 of Appendix 2 shows that the pace of funding under the ENT method is even steeper. This suggests that the ENT method should produce, for new entrants, reserves even exceeding accrued benefits according to the ACC2 definition.

The level of "security" provided in respect of new entrants would be assured in respect of the initial population only when the initial accrued liability has been fully discharged. In other words, at that stage the "unfunded accrued liability" would have been eliminated. The scheme would at that time reach what may be termed the "fully funded" status.

2.8 AGGREGATE COST METHODS

As already mentioned, aggregate cost methods determine the time-related contribution rate function on a collective basis. Among the several possible variants, the following is selected for illustration.

In this variant (Trowbridge and Farr, 1976, p. 55: Tilove, 1976, p. 157), the time-related contribution rate is that level rate which would ensure the closed-fund financial equilibrium of the scheme at that time, taking into account the accumulated reserves. Thus, let

$\text{PVB}(t) =$ present value of future benefits of existing active members (excluding new entrants beyond that time) and existing pensioners;

$\text{PVS}(t) =$ present value of future salaries of existing active members;

$V(t) =$ accumulated reserve fund;

$C(t) =$ time-related contribution rate function. Then,

$$C(t) = \frac{\text{PVB}(t) - V(t)}{\text{PVS}(t)} \qquad (2.16)$$

For a new scheme starting with zero reserves, the contribution rate function will start at AP1 and reduce smoothly and asymptotically to AP2. This variant of the aggregate methods is referred to as AGG.

As compared to the ENT method, the AGG method has the amortization of the initial accrued liability built into the method instead of treating it separately. In effect, the initial accrued liability is being funded through decreasing rather than level amounts. Once this liability is fully discharged, this method would become identical to the ENT method and would be fully funded.

It will be recalled (see section 1.7 of Chapter 1) that the "autonomous funding system" (AFS) achieves the same result as the AGG method, but through a different time-related contribution rate function, over the active lifetime of the initial population. Eventually, when the initial population is fully retired, the AFS becomes identical to ENT and is therefore fully funded at that stage.

The AGG method is illustrated in figures 13 and 14 (page 113) of Appendix 2, in relation to the AFS and ENT systems.

Another version of the aggregate cost method, which corresponds to the system of successive control periods – see section 1.9 of Chapter 1 – is based on forward projections of expenditures and insured salaries, which are established as for social security schemes. The level contribution rate for an interval (n, m), computed at $t = n$ taking into account the reserve in hand, would be such as to produce a terminal reserve which bears a specified ratio to the projected accrued liability at $t = m$. In this manner, the initial accrued liability could be progressively amortized over successive intervals.

2.9 CONCLUSION

This chapter has shown that the funding methods applied to occupational pension schemes are essentially an extension of the family of financing methods applied to social security pension schemes, with the GAP method at the boundary between the two sets of methods.

The occupational pension funding methods aim at attaining the status of full funding in a reasonable, finite period of time, whereas this is not an objective of the social security financing methods. In other words, occupational pension schemes are considerably more pre-funded than social security pension schemes. This translates in practice into contrary patterns of time-related contribution rates and reserve functions. Social security financing methods produce contribution rates which are initially lower than the GAP but eventually higher, whereas occupational pension funding methods generate contribution rates initially higher than the GAP but eventually lower. As a consequence, social security pension schemes generally accumulate lower reserves than the GAP system, while occupational pension schemes accumulate higher reserves.

ADVANCED TOPICS IN SOCIAL SECURITY PENSION FINANCING

3

3.1 INTRODUCTION

This chapter analyses in further detail the characteristics of social security pension schemes and the methods of financing them. The consequences of relaxing the simplifying assumptions made in Chapter 1 are discussed. The effect of the determining parameters is illustrated by considering the sensitivity of selected premiums to changes in parametric values. Finally, the chapter deals with the problem of the indexation of pensions and the constraints arising out of the degree of funding.

3.2 THE PROJECTION AND PRESENT VALUE APPROACHES

There are two actuarial approaches for the analysis of a pension scheme: the projection approach and the present value approach. With reference to the Lexis diagram (figure 1, page 107), the projection approach concentrates on the vertical lines, while the present value approach concentrates on the diagonals. Both approaches, however, lead to the same results or conclusions if they cover the same zone of the Lexis diagram.

The analysis in Chapter 1 was based on the projection approach, the basic elements being the expenditure function $B(t)$ and the insured salary function $S(t)$, introduced in section 1.4. Chapter 2, on the other hand, was based on the present value approach – since the actuarial cost methods discussed in sections 2.2 to 2.4 achieved equilibrium along the diagonals – but the passage in section 2.5 and after to contribution rate and reserve functions dependent on time was implicitly based on the equivalence of the two approaches.

In this chapter recourse will be had to either approach, as required, to analyse the properties of various financial systems.

3.3   EXTENSION OF THE THEORY TO INVALIDITY AND SURVIVORS' PENSIONS

The treatment in Chapter 1 was limited to retirement pensions. Social security pension schemes, however, almost invariably cover the risks of invalidity and death as well, and provide pensions to invalidity pensioners and to survivors (generally, widows/widowers and orphans) of those who die during active service or when in receipt of a retirement or invalidity pension.

Persons involved in a pension scheme can be regarded as constituting several distinct sub-populations. In Chapter 1 the sub-populations of active insured persons and retired persons were introduced. Invalidity pensioners constitute another sub-population which is augmented by new invalids and depleted by deaths of existing invalids. The force of the invalidity decrement, which will apply to persons in the active age range, like the force of mortality, is assumed to be gender and age specific. As in the case of the sub-populations of active persons and retirement pensioners, discussed in section 1.3, the sub-population of invalidity pensioners will, for a new pension scheme, under the assumption of the constancy of the determining parameters, also increase steadily from zero and eventually reach maturity. It will then have a stable age distribution and a constant force of growth equal to that of active persons and retirement pensioners (ρ). However, the time taken to attain this status will be longer. This is because the incremental element, constituted by new invalids, will become stable only when the active population reaches maturity; the youngest invalid created at that time must reach the limit of age before the whole sub-population of invalids becomes stable.

Similar considerations apply to survivors, but the time taken to attain maturity will be even longer. In the case of widows, the incremental element, constituted by new widows, will become stable only when the three sub-populations of active persons, retired persons and invalidity pensioners all become stable; the youngest widow created at that time must reach the limit of age before the sub-population of widows becomes stable. In the case of orphans, the youngest orphan created at the above-mentioned time must reach the maximum age limit for the payment of the orphan's pension.

Thus the inclusion of invalidity and survivors' pensions will not affect the basic trend of the expenditure and salary functions discussed in section 1.4 except that the duration to financial maturity will be correspondingly extended. The theory of social security pension financing developed in Chapter 1 for retirement pensions therefore applies equally to a comprehensive pension scheme providing invalidity and survivors' pensions in addition to retirement pensions.

For demonstration purposes, reference will continue to be made to retirement pensions only, it being generally understood that the results apply also to invalidity and survivors' pensions, unless indicated otherwise.

3.4 MULTIPLE ENTRY AND RETIREMENT AGES

The treatment in Chapter 1 was based on the assumption that all new entrants enter the scheme at a single entry age. However, the same arguments apply to other entry ages and, provided that the force of growth of the number of new entrants (ρ) is the same at all ages, the sum of the results for the various entry ages will display the same characteristic trend.

Again, in Chapter 1 a uniform retirement age was assumed. However, if retirement can take place over a range of ages terminating at a given maximum retirement age, provided that the force of retirement at each age is constant over time, by analogy with the case of invalidity pensions, it can be deduced that retirements occurring over a range of ages will not affect the basic trends and theory developed in Chapter 1.

For demonstration purposes, reference will continue to be made to a single entry age b and to a single retirement age r, it being understood that the results are valid for multiple entry and retirement ages.

3.5 EXPRESSIONS FOR NEW ENTRANT FUNCTIONS

Until a pension scheme reaches financial maturity, its financial development will be influenced by the specific demographic and economic characteristics of the initially insured population. The further discussion of a pension scheme, particularly the analysis of the effect of the determining parameters, is considerably simplified in the financially mature situation, when the initial population has disappeared from the scene. Expressions are developed in this section for various functions relating to new entrants, which apply to the mature situation.

Functions relating to the cohort entering at time t

Let $\{l_x^a\}$, $b \leq x \leq r$, represent the service table for active persons and $\{l_x^p\}$, $r \leq x < \omega$, denote the life table for retired persons, b being the youngest entry age, r the highest retirement age and ω the limit of life.

Consider the new entrants entering at age b and retiring at age r. Let us assume, as in section 1.2, that the number of new entrants in the time interval $(0, dt)$ is dt and that their salary at entry is one unit. Then the new entrants entering in the interval $(t, t + dt)$ will number $e^{\rho t}\, dt$ at entry and their salary at entry will be $e^{\gamma t}$ units, where ρ is the force of growth of new entrants and γ is the force of salary escalation.

The following expressions concern various entities relating to the whole new entrant cohort recruited at time t. They are derived from first principles and then expressed in terms of commutation functions and annuity functions in which the superscripts a and p respectively denote functions relating to active persons and retirees, the superscript s indicates that the salary scale function s_x is incorporated and the superscript in brackets specifies the underlying force of interest.

(a)   The probable present value, at entry, of an annuity of one monetary unit per year, payable from entry to retirement:

$$e^{\rho t} \int_b^r \frac{l_z^a}{l_b^a} e^{-\delta(z-b)}\, dz = e^{\rho t} \bar{a}_{b:\overline{r-b}|}^{a(\delta)} \tag{3.1}$$

(b)   The probable present value, at entry, of an annuity of one monetary unit per year, payable for life after retirement:

$$e^{\rho t} \frac{l_r^a}{l_b^a} e^{-\delta(r-b)} \int_r^\omega \frac{l_z^p}{l_r^p} e^{-\delta(z-r)}\, dz = e^{\rho t} \frac{D_r^{a(\delta)}}{D_b^{a(\delta)}} \bar{a}_r^{p(\delta)} \tag{3.2}$$

(c)   The probable present value, at entry, of insured salaries, allowing for salary progression along a salary scale s_x and for escalation of the general level of salaries with force γ:

$$e^{\rho t} e^{\gamma t} \int_b^r \frac{l_z^a}{l_b^a} \frac{s_z}{s_b} e^{\gamma(z-b)} e^{-\delta(z-b)}\, dz = e^{(\rho+\gamma)t} \bar{a}_{b:\overline{r-b}|}^{as(\delta-\gamma)} \tag{3.3}$$

(d)   The probable present value, at entry, of a retirement pension accruing at 1 per cent of the final salary per year of service, allowing for pension indexation with force β:

$$e^{\rho t} e^{\gamma t} \frac{r-b}{100} \frac{l_r^a}{l_b^a} \frac{s_r}{s_b} e^{\gamma(r-b)} e^{-\delta(r-b)} \int_r^\omega \frac{l_z^p}{l_r^p} e^{\beta(z-r)} e^{-\delta(z-r)}\, dz = \frac{r-b}{100} e^{(\rho+\gamma)t} \frac{D_r^{as(\delta-\gamma)}}{D_b^{as(\delta-\gamma)}} \bar{a}_r^{p(\delta-\beta)} \tag{3.4}$$

Functions relating to the active and retired population existing at time t

In order to obtain the expressions for the active population, denoted by $A(t)$, and the retired population, denoted by $R(t)$, deriving from new entrants entering at age b, and for the corresponding insured salary and benefit expenditure functions $S(t)$ and $B(t)$, it is necessary to regard each of these functions as the integrals of related functions $Ac(x, t)$, $Re(x, t)$, $Sa(x, t)$ and $Be(x, t)$ over the appropriate ranges of x, where x denotes age.

The following expressions for $Ac(x, t)$ and so on are obtained by noting that these are derived from the cohort entering at time $t - (x - b)$ which numbered $e^{\rho(t-x+b)}$ and had a salary of $e^{\gamma(t-x+b)}$ units at entry, and then allowing for: (i) survival from age b to age x – according to the active service table until retirement age r and according to the life table for retirees thereafter; (ii) salary progression according to the salary scale function s_x and due to general salary escalation with force γ until retirement; and (iii) pension indexation after retirement with force β:

(a) Projected number of survivors from $e^{\rho(t-x+b)}$ entrants at age b, to active age x:

$$Ac(x,t) = e^{\rho(t-x+b)} \frac{l_x^a}{l_b^a} = e^{\rho t} \frac{D_x^{a(\rho)}}{D_b^{a(\rho)}} \tag{3.5}$$

(b) Projected salary amount of the $Ac(x,t)$ persons, starting from a unit salary at age x, which is adjusted according to the salary scale function s_x and escalated with force γ:

$$Sa(x,t) = Ac(x,t) \frac{s_x}{s_b} e^{\gamma t} = e^{(\rho+\gamma)t} \frac{D_x^{as(\rho)}}{D_b^{as(\rho)}} \tag{3.6}$$

(c) Projected number of survivors from $e^{\rho(t-x+b)}$ entrants at age b, to pension age x:

$$Re(x,t) = e^{\rho(t-x+b)} \frac{l_r^a}{l_b^a} \frac{l_x^p}{l_r^p} = e^{\rho t} \frac{D_r^{a(\rho)}}{D_b^{a(\rho)}} \frac{D_x^{p(\rho)}}{D_r^{p(\rho)}} \tag{3.7}$$

(d) Projected pension amount of the $Re(x,t)$ persons, computed at $(r-b)$ per cent of the salary – at retirement age r – resulting from the unit salary at entry age b adjusted according to the salary scale function s_x and escalated with force γ, such pension being indexed with force β:

$$Be(x,t) = Re(x,t) \frac{r-b}{100} \frac{s_r}{s_b} e^{\gamma(t-x+r)} e^{\beta(x-r)} = \frac{r-b}{100} e^{(\rho+\gamma)t} \frac{D_r^{as(\rho)}}{D_b^{as(\rho)}} \frac{D_x^{p(\rho+\gamma-\beta)}}{D_r^{p(\rho+\gamma-\beta)}} \tag{3.8}$$

Integrating the functions $Ac(x,t)$ and $Sa(x,t)$ with respect to x over the range (b,r) and the functions $Re(x,t)$ and $Be(x,t)$ over the range (r,ω), the following expressions are obtained:

(a) Total number of active lives at time t:

$$A(t) = e^{\rho t} \, \bar{a}_{b:r-b|}^{a(\rho)} \tag{3.9}$$

(b) Total number of pensioners at time t:

$$R(t) = e^{\rho t} \frac{D_r^{a(\rho)}}{D_b^{a(\rho)}} \bar{a}_r^{p(\rho)} \tag{3.9}$$

(c) Total amount of salaries at time t:

$$S(t) = e^{(\rho+\gamma)t} \, \bar{a}_{b:r-b|}^{as(\rho)} \tag{3.11}$$

(d) Total amount of pensions at time t:

$$B(t) = e^{(\rho+\gamma)t} \frac{r-b}{100} \frac{D_r^{as(\rho)}}{D_b^{as(\rho)}} \bar{a}_r^{p(\rho+\gamma-\beta)} \tag{3.12}$$

The symbol $\bar{a}_{x:\bar{n}|}^{as(\alpha)}$ – occurring in (3.3) and (3.11) – represents a continuous, fixed-term annuity, based on the service table for active persons and on force of interest α, the amount of the annuity increasing from unity in line with the salary scale function.

It will be apparent from the functional forms of the above expressions that, in the mature situation, $A(t)$ and $R(t)$ grow at the instantaneous rate ρ and $S(t)$ and $B(t)$ grow at the instantaneous rate $\rho + \gamma$, thus confirming the findings based on general reasoning in sections 1.3 and 1.4.

Relationship between functions relating to the population existing at time t and functions relating to entrants at time t

It will be noted that the expressions for the demographic projections at time t – (3.9) and (3.10) – have the same structure as those of unitary annuities payable to the new entrants recruited at time t – (3.1) and (3.2) – except that the underlying force of interest is ρ instead of δ. Further, the expressions for the financial projections at time t – (3.11) and (3.12) – have the same structure as those for the present values of salaries and benefits of the new entrants recruited at time t – (3.3) and (3.4) – except that ρ replaces $\delta - \gamma$. These results, which have been established above for retirement benefits and for the specific pension formula, are in fact particular cases of more general theorems which apply also to invalidity and survivors' benefits and for any pension formula (Thullen, 1973, pp. VIII-4 to VIII-11).

3.6 PREMIUMS IN THE FINANCIALLY MATURE SITUATION

Limiting the consideration again to the single entry age b and to the single retirement age r, the pay-as-you-go premium in the mature situation (PAYG*) is obtained by dividing (3.12) by (3.11):

$$\text{PAYG}^* = \frac{r-b}{100} \frac{D_r^{as(\rho)}}{D_b^{as(\rho)}} \frac{\bar{a}_r^{p(\rho+\gamma-\beta)}}{\bar{a}_{b:r-b|}^{as(\rho)}}$$

The average premium for new entrants (denoted by AP2* for consistency with the notation in section 1.7) is obtained by dividing (3.4) by (3.3):

$$\text{AP2}^* = \frac{r-b}{100} \frac{D_r^{as(\delta-\gamma)}}{D_b^{as(\delta-\gamma)}} \frac{\bar{a}_r^{p(\delta-\beta)}}{\bar{a}_{b:r-b|}^{as(\delta-\gamma)}} \qquad (3.14)$$

The terminal funding premium in the mature situation (TFS*) is obtained by multiplying the number of persons retiring in the interval $(t, t+dt)$

$$e^{\rho t} \cdot \frac{D_r^{a(\rho)}}{D_b^{a(\rho)}} \, dt \qquad (3.15)$$

by the retirement capital required per retiree,

$$e^{\gamma t} \frac{r-b}{100} \frac{s_r}{s_b} \bar{a}_r^{p(\delta-\beta)} \tag{3.16}$$

which, after division by $S(t)\,dt$ and simplification, gives

$$\text{TFS}^* = \frac{r-b}{100} \frac{D_r^{as(\rho)}}{D_b^{as(\rho)}} \frac{\bar{a}_r^{p(\delta-\beta)}}{\bar{a}_{b:\overline{r-b|}}^{as(\rho)}} \tag{3.17}$$

The similarity of the structure of the three premiums is noteworthy. This result, which has been established here for retirement pensions, for single entry and retirement ages, and for a specific pension formula, can be generalized to invalidity and survivors' pensions, to multiple entry and retirement ages and to any pension formula (ibid., pp. VIII-11 to VIII-15).

It will be observed from (3.13), (3.14) and (3.17) that:

- the pay-as-you-go premium depends on ρ, γ and β but is independent of δ;
- the average new entrant premium depends on δ, γ and β but is independent of ρ;
- the terminal funding premium depends on ρ, δ and β but is independent of γ.

In order to judge the effect on each premium of an increase or decrease in any of the relevant parameters, it is convenient to consider the structure of the premium formula – apart from the pension rate $(r-b)/100$ – in two parts. The first component, which relates to the active service, can be written as

$$\frac{D_r^{as(\alpha)}}{D_b^{as(\alpha)}} \frac{1}{\bar{a}_{b:\overline{r-b|}}^{as(\alpha)}} = \frac{l_r^a s_r\, e^{-\alpha r}}{\int_b^r l_z^a s_z\, e^{-\alpha z}\, dz} \tag{3.18}$$

where α denotes the relevant force of interest. From the right hand side, it will be seen that if α is increased, the exponential factor in the numerator will reduce relatively more than the exponential factor in the integrand in the denominator, so that this component of the premium formula will reduce.

A similar argument applies to the second component of the premium formula,

$$\bar{a}_r^{p(\alpha)} = \frac{\int_r^\omega l_z^p\, e^{-\alpha z}\, dz}{l_r^p\, e^{-\alpha r}} \tag{3.19}$$

Thus any change in the parameters leading to an increase in any of the underlying forces of interest will lead to a decrease in the premiums and vice versa. The following conclusions can therefore be reached:

- if ρ is increased, PAYG* and TFS* will decrease, but AP2* will be unaffected;
- if γ is increased, PAYG* will decrease and AP2* will increase, but TFS* will be unaffected;

- if δ is increased, AP2* and TFS* will decrease, but PAYG* will be unaffected;
- if β is increased, all three of PAYG*, AP2* and TFS* will increase.

The case $\beta = \gamma$ (wage indexation) is of particular interest. In this case, it will be seen that the premiums depend only on ρ and the difference $\delta - \gamma$ (sometimes called the *real rate of interest*, in relation to salary escalation). In this case the following observations can be made:

- if ρ is increased, PAYG* and TFS* will decrease, but AP2* will be unaffected;
- if the real rate of interest $(\delta - \gamma)$ is increased, PAYG* is unaffected, but TFS* and AP2* will reduce. However, TFS* is less sensitive than PAYG* to changes in ρ and less sensitive than AP2* to changes in $\delta - \gamma$ (ibid., p. IX-19).

The effects on the various premiums of variations in individual parameters, both when $\gamma > \beta$ and $\gamma = \beta$, are demonstrated numerically in table 7 of Appendix 2 (page 106) for the hypothetical pension scheme.

An important deduction which can be made by comparing the expressions for PAYG* and AP2* is that if $\delta - \gamma < \rho$ (i.e. $\delta < \rho + \gamma$), then the unfunded pay-as-you-go premium will be lower than the funded new entrant average premium. To make funding worthwhile, therefore, the force of interest should exceed the sum of the force of growth of new entrants and the force of salary escalation. This is the condition which was mentioned in section 1.2.

3.7   ANALYSIS OF THE GENERAL AVERAGE PREMIUM

Consider first the case of wage indexation $(\beta = \gamma)$. Let the general average premium corresponding to this case be denoted by GAP*. Since pensions are always in line with the level of salaries, the expenditure function – including administration costs, under the assumptions stated at the end of section 1.4 of Chapter 1 – and the insured salary function take the form

$$B(t) = B^*(t)\,e^{\gamma t} \quad \text{and} \quad S(t) = S^*(t)\,e^{\gamma t}$$

where $B^*(t)$ and $S^*(t)$ do not involve γ. The general average premium (see equation (1.14) of Chapter 1) can therefore be expressed as

$$\text{GAP}^* = \frac{\int_0^\infty B^*(t)\,e^{-(\delta-\gamma)t}\,dt}{\int_0^\infty S^*(t)\,e^{-(\delta-\gamma)t}\,dt} = \frac{\int_0^\infty B^*(t)\,e^{-\phi t}\,dt}{\int_0^\infty S^*(t)\,e^{-\phi t}\,dt} \tag{3.20}$$

where ϕ denotes the real rate of interest. The effect on GAP* of changes in the real rate of interest can be investigated by partially differentiating the above expression with respect to ϕ (ρ being held constant) and considering the sign of the differential coefficient. The expression for the partial differential coefficient is as follows:

$$\frac{\partial(\text{GAP}^*)}{\partial\phi} = \text{GAP}^*(\text{ADTS} - \text{ADTB}) \tag{3.21}$$

where ADTS and ADTB, respectively, denote the average discounted terms of $S(t)$ and $B(t)$ and are given by

$$\text{ADTS} = \frac{\int_0^\infty tS(t)\,e^{-\delta t}\,dt}{\int_0^\infty S(t)\,e^{-\delta t}\,dt} \tag{3.22}$$

$$\text{ADTB} = \frac{\int_0^\infty tB(t)\,e^{-\delta t}\,dt}{\int_0^\infty B(t)\,e^{-\delta t}\,dt} \tag{3.23}$$

It can therefore be concluded that GAP^* will decrease when the real rate of interest is increased, subject to the condition that the average discounted term of the function $B(t)$ is greater than that of the function $S(t)$. It will be noted that if $B(t)$ and $S(t)$ have the characteristics mentioned at the end of section 1.4, then their average discounted terms will meet the above condition. It is assumed in what follows that $\text{ADTB} > \text{ADTS}$.

The general case $(\beta \neq \gamma)$ is complex, but considering retirement pensions alone and a single retirement age r, the general average premium can be expressed as

$$\text{GAP} = [\text{GAP}^*]\,\frac{\bar{a}_r^{p(\delta - \beta)}}{\bar{a}_r^{p(\delta - \gamma)}} \tag{3.24}$$

This will be evident if the numerator of GAP is regarded as the sum of the probable present values of the pension expenditures of individual cohorts. Let f denote the second factor on the right-hand side of (3.24). Let ADT1 and ADT2 represent the average discounted terms of the annuities in the numerator and denominator of f. It can be shown that, provided $\beta < \gamma$, $\text{ADT2} > \text{ADT1}$. The partial differential coefficients of GAP with respect to δ and γ can be expressed as

$$\frac{\partial(\text{GAP})}{\partial\delta} = \text{GAP}[-(\text{ADTB} - \text{ADTS}) + (\text{ADT2} - \text{ADT1})]$$

$$\frac{\partial(\text{GAP})}{\partial\gamma} = \text{GAP}[\text{ADTB} - \text{ADTS} - \text{ADT2}] \tag{3.25}$$

The first expression of (3.25) indicates that, subject to the condition $\text{ADTB} - \text{ADTS} > \text{ADT2} - \text{ADT1}$, an increase in δ leads to a decrease in GAP. The second expression indicates that an increase in γ will lead to an increase in GAP, subject to the condition $\text{ADTB} - \text{ADTS} > \text{ADT2}$. Since GAP^* and the denominator of f are both independent of β, it is evident from (3.24) that an increase in β will lead to an increase in GAP.

To analyse the effect on the general average premium of changes in the force of growth of new entrants (ρ), consider equation (1.17) of Chapter 1. The part concerning the initial insured population obviously does not depend on ρ. AP2 will also not be affected by a change in ρ – see section 3.6, above. An increase in ρ will, however, increase the salaries of new entrants and therefore increase the weight of AP2 in equation (1.17). This will lead to a decrease in GAP since $\text{AP2} < \text{AP1}$.

The effect of changes in the parameters on GAP and GAP* is illustrated in table 7 of Appendix 2. With reference to GAP*, it will be noted that a decrease in the real rate of interest can be compensated by an increase in the force of recruitment of new entrants. This is an aspect of the interchangeability of biometric and economic parameters (Zelenka, 1959).

3.8 RESERVES IN THE FINANCIALLY MATURE SITUATION

If financial maturity is attained at $t = \omega_2$, the following relationship holds between the reserve at the onset of maturity and the level premium π required in the mature situation:

$$V(\omega_2) = \frac{B(\omega_2) - \pi S(\omega_2)}{\delta - \rho - \gamma} \tag{3.26}$$

The above result was proved in section 1.9; it is valid, subject to the condition $\delta > \rho + \gamma$, for any financial system which applies a level premium during maturity. Further, it can be shown that the reserve at any subsequent time $t = \omega_2 + z$ is given by $V(\omega_2 + z) = V(\omega_2) e^{(\rho + \gamma)z}$. Thus once financial maturity is attained, the reserve function grows at the same pace as the benefit and salary functions.

The system reserve function can be expressed as follows in terms of the system premium and the pay-as-you-go premium in the mature situation:

$$V(t)(\delta - \rho - \gamma) = S(t)(\text{PAYG}^* - \pi) \tag{3.27}$$

This also implies that the higher the system premium, the lower the system reserves in the mature situation, a phenomenon which was consistently observed in the illustrations of the financial systems in Chapters 1 and 2.

3.9 THE EFFECT OF MORTALITY AND INVALIDITY DECREMENTS

The active population is subject to two decrements: mortality and invalidity. The retired population is subject to the mortality decrement only. The force of each decrement will be gender and age specific. In this section, the effect on the premiums (for retirement benefits) of assuming higher levels of mortality (or invalidity) is discussed.

Let the forces of the mortality and the invalidity decrements at age x be denoted by μ_x^d and μ_x^i. Then the active service table function ($b \leq x \leq r$) is given by

$$l_x^a = l_b^a \exp\left(-\int_b^x (\mu_z^d + \mu_z^i)\, dz\right) \tag{3.28}$$

This shows that the effect of an increase in the force of invalidity is equivalent to the same increase in the force of mortality at the same age.

Reference is now made to the important result that an increase in the rate of mortality is equivalent to an increase in the rate of interest (Jordan, 1967, pp. 56–57). Thus an increase in either the force of invalidity or the force of mortality over the active service age range (b, r) should produce the same effect as an increase in the force of interest over this range, and an increase in the force of mortality after retirement should produce the same effect as an increase in the force of interest over the age-range (r, ω). Thus, an increase in either the force of mortality or the force of invalidity will lead to a decrease in the premiums.

It should be noted, however, that the above-mentioned effect of the mortality and invalidity decrements apply only to premiums relating to retirement pensions. The effect on the premium relating to survivors' pensions of a higher force of mortality will be contrary, and so will be the effect on the premium for invalidity pensions of a higher force of invalidity. This produces a mutually compensating effect in a comprehensive social security pension scheme covering all three risks of retirement, invalidity and death (Thullen, 1973, p. IX-7 and IX-10).

3.10   THE EFFECT OF THE DENSITY FACTOR

The density factor was defined in section 1.2 as the proportion of potential time that members in the active age range are effectively contributing to the scheme. Hitherto, the density was assumed uniformly at 100 per cent at all ages. The effect on the premiums discussed in section 3.6, of a lower density, possibly varying by age, is considered in this section. (The possibility of service credits during non-contributory periods, for example during sickness, is ignored here). It is recognized that there are also other similar factors affecting contribution income, such as evasion or underdeclaration of contributory earnings, but they are not discussed here.

Let $\lambda(x)$ denote the proportion of insured persons who are effectively in contributory service at age x. Assuming that the density factor uniformly affects all individuals of a given age, the total contributory service of a new entrant at age b on reaching retirement age r would be $\int_b^r \lambda(x)\, dx$. It can be shown that the effect of a different density assumption is to alter the premium AP2* for 100 per cent density by the factor λ_1 / λ_2 and the corresponding PAYG* and TFS* premiums by the factor λ_1 / λ_3, where λ_1, λ_2 and λ_3 are averages of $\lambda(x)$ over the age range (b, r) given by

$$\lambda_1 = \frac{\int_b^r \lambda(x)\, dx}{r - b} \tag{3.29}$$

$$\lambda_2 = \frac{\int_b^r D_x^{as(\delta - \gamma)} \lambda(x)\, dx}{\int_b^r D_x^{as(\delta - \gamma)}\, dx} \tag{3.30}$$

47

$$\lambda_3 = \frac{\int_b^r D_x^{as(\rho)} \lambda(x)\, dx}{\int_b^r D_x^{as(\rho)}\, dx} \tag{3.31}$$

It would appear that, even if the density differs from 100 per cent, provided that it does not vary by age, $\lambda_1 = \lambda_2 = \lambda_3$; the premiums are not affected. If density does vary by age, the exact effect on PAYG*, TFS* and AP2* will depend on the nature of the functions $\lambda(x)$, $D_x^{as(\rho)}$ and $D_x^{as(\delta - \gamma)}$. For example, if $\lambda(x)$ is an increasing function of x and the salary scale function is flat, then λ_1 is likely to be greater than λ_2 and λ_3 so that all the three premiums will increase.

3.11 THE IMPLICATION OF THE FUNDING LEVEL FOR PENSION INDEXATION

For the purposes of this section, the forces of interest and salary escalation are regarded as functions of time, $\delta(t)$ and $\gamma(t)$. In equations (3.14) and (3.17), if β is put equal to γ, the expressions for AP2* and TFS* will involve only the difference $\delta - \gamma$. This will also be the case with the GAP* – see equation (3.20). Therefore, provided that an increase in the force of salary escalation $\gamma(t)$ is compensated by a corresponding increase in the force of interest $\delta(t)$, this will leave their difference unchanged. It would therefore be possible to continue to provide wage indexation without requiring any change in premiums computed on the basis of a given real interest rate. The consequences of the more common phenomenon of an increase in salary escalation without an equal compensating increase in the interest rate is discussed below (ibid., pp. X-4 to X-6).

To be specific, consider an isolated, unanticipated, proportionate increase k in insured salaries at time t. This will have a repercussion on all future salaries, which will all increase in the same proportion. Let k_1 represent the proportionate adjustment which can be given to future pensions. The following are the equations of equilibrium just before and just after the salary increase:

$$V(t)\, e^{-\delta t} = \int_t^\infty B(z)\, e^{-\delta z}\, dz - \int_t^\infty C(z) S(z)\, e^{-\delta z}\, dz \tag{3.32}$$

$$V(t)\, e^{-\delta t} = (1 + k_1) \int_t^\infty B(z)\, e^{-\delta z}\, dz - (1 + k) \int_t^\infty C(z) S(z)\, e^{-\delta z}\, dz \tag{3.33}$$

Combining the two equations and simplifying,

$$\frac{k_1}{k} = 1 - \frac{V(t)\, e^{-\delta t}}{\int_t^\infty B(z)\, e^{-\delta z}\, dz} \tag{3.34}$$

It is seen that in general, $0 < k_1 < k$. Moreover, the lower the reserve function $V(t)$, the higher the ratio k_1/k. Only when $V(t) = 0$, that is when the financial system is pay-as-you-go, is $k_1 = k$ and pensions can be fully adjusted to this isolated increase in salaries.

If a distinction is made between pensions in payment at time t and those to be awarded in the future, and if any increase in insured salaries automatically raises pensions to be awarded in the same proportion because of the pension formula – for example, because the pension is based on the final salary – let k_2 represent the proportionate increase which can be given to existing pensions. The equation of equilibrium after the increase in salaries will then be as follows:

$$V(t)\,e^{-\delta t} = (1+k) \int_t^\infty B_a(z)\,e^{-\delta z}\,dz + (1+k_2) \int_t^\infty B_b(z)\,e^{-\delta z}\,dz$$

$$-\,(1+k) \int_t^\infty C(z)S(z)\,e^{-\delta z}\,dz \qquad (3.35)$$

where $B_b(z)$ denotes the expenditure at time z on pensions in payment at time t and $B_a(z)$ denotes the expenditure on pensions to be awarded after time t. Denoting the reserve for pensioners at time t by $V_b(t)$ and that for active persons by $V_a(t)$ where $V_a(t) + V_b(t) = V(t)$, combining with equation (3.32) and simplifying, the following relationship is obtained:

$$\frac{k_2}{k} = -\frac{V_a(t)}{V_b(t)} \qquad (3.36)$$

This shows that only if the reserve for active persons is negative (i.e. $V(t) < V_b(t)$ meaning that the financial system involves lower funding than the terminal funding system) will it be possible to provide any adjustment to existing pensions.

Hence the level of funding acts as a constraint to pension indexation. This might appear somewhat paradoxical, but the explanation is that funding is supposed to make advance provision for future pension expenditures, including the cost of indexation. The lack of provision in the past in respect of pension adjustment for unanticipated salary escalation shows up in the form of a shortfall in reserves. Although future salaries – and therefore contributions – do increase proportionately, this is not adequate to make up for the shortfall in the reserves, and consequently allows only a partial adjustment of pensions. It is of course possible to cover the shortfall by increasing future contributions or by augmenting the reserves through the injection of additional funds, but this means that there is a departure from the original plan. Only the PAYG system can withstand the effects of unanticipated salary increases without modifying the contribution rates.

On the other hand, the pay-as-you-go system is vulnerable to unanticipated demographic changes. For example, if the force of growth of new entrants, after being constant at a level ρ drops to a lower level ρ_1 over m years and then remains constant, this will cause the PAYG* premium pertaining to retirement pensions to increase over a period of $\omega + m - b$ years, whereas the average premium for new entrants AP2* will be unaffected (Iyer and McGillivray, 1988, pp. 35–36).

3.12 FURTHER GENERALIZATION OF THE THEORY

The theory developed in Chapter 1 and the present chapter can be generalized further. Some possible directions are mentioned in this section, but are not developed in detail.

Additional population decrements or increments

The theory developed so far has considered only two decrements, mortality and invalidity, of the insured active population. In certain circumstances it may be necessary to allow for additional decrements, in particular if there are distinct provisions in regard to the pension benefit. For example, active persons exiting from insured status owing to industrial injury may need to be distinguished separately. Withdrawal from the pension scheme before reaching retirement age is an important decrement for occupational pensions, but is not generally relevant to a social security pension scheme operating at the national level. In any case, the extension to three or more decrements can be handled through the application of multiple decrement theory (see Appendix 1).

A variation on the concept of decrements is that of reactivation of the invalid population, that is, a reverse movement from the invalid group towards the active insured group. In effect, the invalid group is then subject to two decrements (death and reactivation), while the active group is subject to two decrements (death and invalidity) and two increments (new entries and reactivation). For the treatment of reactivation, see Thullen, 1973, pp. II-16 and II-17.

Parametric variation over time

It has been assumed thus far that the determining parameters do not vary over time. However, it is possible to incorporate such a variation. For example, if the force of interest δ is regarded as a function of time, the fundamental equation of equilibrium – equation (1.7) – would be written as follows:

$$\int_0^\infty C(z)S(z)\exp\left(-\int_0^Z \delta(u)\,du\right)dz = \int_0^\infty B(z)\exp\left(-\int_0^Z \delta(u)\,du\right)dz \qquad (3.37)$$

Other parameters can be treated similarly. Specific functional forms of the parameter – more complex, for example, than the simple $\delta(u) = $ constant – could be investigated. However, the mathematical manipulation of the expressions is liable to be complicated. It would therefore be more practicable to use computer simulation methods, such as those discussed in Part II of this book, to study the effect of variation in parameters over time.

Generalization of the concept of maturity

The demographic and financial maturity discussed so far, based on constant parameters ρ and γ, relates to what is termed a "stable" mature situation which implies that all the demographic and financial aggregates are growing exponentially. (If $\rho = \gamma = 0$, the mature situation is described as "absolutely stationary"; the demographic and financial aggregates will then be constant over time).

A more general concept is that of a "relatively stationary" mature situation (ibid., pp. V-4 and V-17). A pension scheme is defined to be in a "relatively stationary" demographic situation if the relative age distributions of the active insured and retired populations are constant, without these populations necessarily growing exponentially. In symbols, the functions $Ac(x, t)$ and $Re(x, t)$ – denoting respectively the active and retired populations aged x at time t – are of the form $\psi(t)L(x)$, where $\psi(t)$ is any function of t. If $\psi(t)$ is an exponential function, we have the case of the "stable" demographically mature situation – see equations (3.5) and (3.7).

A scheme is said to be in a "relatively stationary" financial situation if the benefit expenditure function, the salary function and the reserve function are all growing at the same instantaneous rate, without this rate being necessarily constant over time. Symbolically,

$$\frac{B'(t)}{B(t)} = \frac{S'(t)}{S(t)} = \frac{V'(t)}{V(t)} = \zeta(t) \tag{3.38}$$

where $\zeta(t)$ is any function of t. If $\zeta(t)$ is a constant $(\rho + \gamma)$, we have the case of the "stable" financially mature situation – see equations (3.11) and (3.12).

The stochastic approach

As already indicated in Chapter 1, sections 1.3 and 1.4, the approach taken in this book is *deterministic*. This means that, given the underlying parameters, the outcome in terms of the actuarial functions is taken as uniquely determined. Under the *stochastic* approach the resulting value of an actuarial function is regarded only as the average or expected value of the outcome. The actual outcome has a probability distribution, hence its precise value is uncertain. However, probabilistic statements can be made about the function if the variance of the distribution can be determined.

To take an elementary example, consider the number of deaths occurring in one year out of a known initial number of l_x persons at age x, given the probability of death q_x. In the deterministic approach, the number of deaths is taken as the unique number $d_x = l_x q_x$. In the stochastic approach, the number of deaths, say y, is regarded as a random variable whose expected value (μ) is given by $l_x q_x$. In this simple case, the distribution of y can be seen to be the binomial distribution; hence the variance of the distribution (σ^2) will be given by $l_x q_x(1 - q_x)$. Using the normal approximation, it can then be stated, for example, that

$$\text{Probability}(\mu - 1.96\sigma < y < \mu + 1.96\sigma) = 0.95 \tag{3.39}$$

Actuarial functions are usually complex functions involving several variables. Although the probability distribution of each variable is known, it is generally not possible analytically to derive the probability distribution of the function itself and thus to obtain an algebraic expression for its variance. The solution then is to carry out multiple simulations of the whole process and to estimate the variance from the results. Each simulation involves the drawing of a random value of each variable occurring in the actuarial function.

Stochastic methods have been widely applied in general and life insurance (Bowers et al., 1997; Daykin et al., 1994), but have seen only limited application in the field of pensions (see, however, Daykin et al., 1994, pp. 435–451).

3.13   CONCLUDING REMARKS

In concluding this treatment of the financing of social security pensions, the important long-term relationship between the forces of interest, demographic growth and salary escalation (i.e. $\delta > \rho + \gamma$), mentioned in section 1.2, is recalled and stressed. In fact, this condition has repeatedly appeared at various stages in Chapter 1 and in the present chapter. If this condition did not hold, several integrals intervening in the theoretical development would not converge.

Another important point concerns the implications of the parametric assumptions for the growth of the expenditure and insured salary functions, $B(t)$ and $S(t)$. The assumption that the forces of growth ρ and γ continue indefinitely into the future imply – see sections 1.4 and 3.5 – that once financial maturity is attained, the functions $B(t)$ and $S(t)$ would grow with force $\rho + \gamma$ indefinitely into the future. This could, however, be questioned on common-sensical grounds since the size of these aggregates resulting from such unchecked exponential growth could at some stage conceivably outstrip the resources available to sustain them. It might therefore be more logical to expect the growth rate to slow down and for these aggregates to stabilize.

In this regard, it will be noted that what intervenes in the various integrals is not these aggregates themselves but rather their discounted values. Given the condition $\delta > \rho + \gamma$, the contribution of the expenditure and insured salary functions to the integrals in fact decreases exponentially so that in any case they become insignificant in course of time. Thus the theory which has been developed is not inconsistent with an eventual asymptotic stabilization of the financial aggregates.

DEFINED CONTRIBUTION SCHEMES

4

4.1 INTRODUCTION

Chapters 1 to 3 were concerned with what is termed "defined benefit" schemes. In these schemes, the benefit formula is specified in advance and the financial system, including the schedule of contributions, is then determined so as to ensure the financial equilibrium of the scheme.

This chapter is concerned with "defined contribution" schemes, where the sequence of designing benefits and then contributions is reversed. Thus, the rate of contribution is fixed in advance, and the benefit becomes the dependent variable. Each member's contributions are accumulated in an individual account, with interest or investment return, and the balance in the account is paid out either as a lump sum, or in the form of an annuity, on the occurrence of one of the covered contingencies, that is, retirement, invalidity or death in service.

There are also instances of hybrid schemes where there is a defined benefit, but it is calculated by a formula which derives from the contributions paid or where the benefit is the better of a defined contribution calculation and a defined benefit. Another variant is the "notional defined contribution scheme". This chapter will, however, be mainly concerned with straightforward defined contribution schemes operating at the national level. This includes the so-called national provident funds and a relatively recent innovation, the mandatory retirement savings scheme.

4.2 ACTUARIAL STRUCTURE

From an actuarial point of view the structure of defined contribution schemes is simple, although methods for attributing the investment return to individual accounts may be relatively complex. There are no systematic cross-subsidies within or between generations during the funding stage, since members are entitled to the invested accumulation (or an approximation thereto) of what they have paid in (or has been paid in on their behalf). The only elements of insurance relate to arrangements made to secure benefits on invalidity or death before normal retirement age, as well as the insurance against longevity where annuities are paid over the retired lifetime of pensioners.

As regards the determining parameters – see section 1.2 of Chapter 1 – the forces of interest, salary escalation and inflation (δ, γ and θ) are particularly relevant to the discussion of the financial aspects of defined contribution schemes. In a defined contribution scheme, the benefit is determined, apart from the contributions themselves, by the interest or investment return credited to the individual accounts, while the successive contributions are determined by the member's salary progression. On the other hand, the real value of the benefit will be affected by inflation over the contributory career. The risks associated with these factors, in particular the risk that the investment returns may not keep up with inflation over the period of membership, are borne by the individual member. This contrasts with the case of a defined benefit scheme, where these risks are borne by the sponsor of an occupational plan, or collectively by all contributors to a social security pension scheme.

With regard to the financial system, unlike a defined benefit scheme, there is no question of a choice, since by its very definition, a defined contribution scheme is necessarily fully funded on an individual basis. Moreover, to make the ultimate benefit meaningful, it is usually necessary to have a relatively high contribution rate from the outset unless an age-related contribution schedule is specified, which might involve quite high levels of contribution as retirement age approaches. Consequently, a defined contribution social security scheme does not have the flexibility of adapting the reserve accumulation to the investment needs and the absorptive capacity of the national economy, a possibility for defined benefit schemes (see section 1.11). In addition, the transparency of the arrangement for the attribution of investment return to individual accounts (normally reported to members at least once a year) tends to constrain investment policy to avoid the possibility of negative returns in the short term, even if this means forgoing the potential for a higher return in the long term.

The maturing process of a newly introduced defined contribution scheme is similar to that of a new defined benefit scheme, described in section 1.4 (Iyer, 1971). Under the simplified assumptions of Chapter 1, including the constancy of the determining parameters, a national provident fund providing lump-sum retirement benefits only would attain financial maturity when the youngest initial entrant reached retirement age. A corresponding mandatory retirement savings scheme which pays annuities in lieu of lump sums would attain financial maturity when the youngest initial entrant reached the limit of life.

4.3 ANALYSIS OF THE ACCUMULATED BALANCE

For the purposes of this chapter, it is proposed to introduce the parameter γ^*, which represents the force of growth of the salary of a participant, assumed constant throughout his or her career. It represents the combined effect of general salary escalation (γ) and progression of the member's salary due to advancing seniority (the salary scale effect). Thus, γ^* would generally be greater than γ and may exceed δ.

Taking the starting annual salary as one monetary unit and the contribution density as 100 per cent, the accumulated balance after a contributory career of n years will be given by

$$\pi \int_0^n e^{\gamma^* z} e^{\delta(n-z)} \, dz = \pi e^{n\delta} \bar{s}_{\bar{n}|}^{(\gamma^* - \delta)} = \pi e^{n\gamma^*} \bar{a}_{\bar{n}|}^{(\gamma^* - \delta)} \tag{4.1}$$

The accumulated balance can also be expressed as

$$\pi e^{n\delta} \bar{a}_{\bar{n}|}^{(\delta - \gamma^*)} = \pi e^{n\gamma^*} \bar{s}_{\bar{n}|}^{(\delta - \gamma^*)} \tag{4.2}$$

where π represents the contribution rate. Mathematically, all four expressions are acceptable although (4.1) may be preferred when γ^* is greater than δ and (4.2) in the case where $\delta > \gamma^*$. This is, however, only a matter of presentation and both forms $\delta - \gamma^*$ and $\gamma^* - \delta$ are used in the following development.

It is useful to relate the accumulated balance to the final annual salary, $e^{n\gamma^*}$, which represents the member's earning power just before retirement. This gives the following result for the relative accumulated balance, that is, the balance as a multiple of the final salary:

$$\pi \bar{a}_{\bar{n}|}^{(\gamma^* - \delta)} \tag{4.3}$$

This shows that the relative accumulated balance depends only on the difference $\gamma^* - \delta$. The lower this difference (i.e. the higher δ relative to γ^*), the higher the relative accumulated balance.

The total nominal amount of the contributions (excluding interest) is given by

$$\pi \int_0^n e^{\gamma^* z} \, dz = \pi e^{n\gamma^*} \bar{a}_{\bar{n}|}^{(\gamma^*)} \tag{4.4}$$

By dividing (4.2) by (4.4), the accumulated balance can be expressed as a multiple of the sum of the contributions, which shows the relative importance of the interest element in the balance

$$\frac{\bar{a}_{\bar{n}|}^{(\gamma^* - \delta)}}{\bar{a}_{\bar{n}|}^{(\gamma^*)}} \tag{4.5}$$

The above expression, however, relates to monetary amounts and is therefore in nominal terms. In order to pass to "real" terms, it is necessary to discount both the accumulated balance (4.2) and the integrand on the left-hand side of (4.4) for inflation. This gives the following expression for the "real" balance as a multiple of the sum of "real" contributions:

$$\frac{\bar{a}_{\overline{n}|}^{(\gamma^{*}-\delta)}}{\bar{a}_{\overline{n}|}^{(\gamma^{*}-\theta)}} \tag{4.6}$$

By noting that the higher the underlying force of interest, the lower the value of the annuity, it can be seen that the condition for (4.5) to exceed unity is $\delta > 0$; and the condition for (4.6) to exceed unity is $\delta > \theta$. If $0 < \delta < \theta$, (4.5) will exceed unity but (4.6) will be less than unity. In this case the member, although apparently receiving an addition to his or her contributions in the form of interest, actually suffers a loss in real terms on contributions to the scheme, that is, earns a negative real rate of return.

4.4   ANALYSIS OF THE RETIREMENT ANNUITY

If the balance is converted into an annuity at, say, age x, the replacement rate, that is, the initial amount of the annuity as a percentage of the terminal salary, will be obtained by dividing (4.3) by the appropriate annuity factor. The simplest case is where the annuity is payable for m years certain and is not indexed. The replacement rate is then given by

$$\pi \frac{\bar{a}_{\overline{n}|}^{(\gamma^{*}-\delta)}}{\bar{a}_{\overline{m}|}^{(\delta)}} \tag{4.7}$$

If the annuity is to be indexed with force β, then the annuity factor in the denominator should refer to force $(\delta - \beta)$, which will lead to a lower replacement rate. This illustrates an important difference between defined contribution and defined benefit schemes; in the latter schemes, indexation of the pension, if provided for, generally forms part of the benefit package, whereas in the former, indexation has to be traded off against a lower replacement rate.

The balance can be converted into an indexed life annuity by using the annuity factor $\bar{a}_{x}^{(\delta-\beta)}$. A survivors' element can be added by modifying the annuity factor. For example, a spouse's annuity equal to a proportion k of the retirement annuity can be accommodated by replacing the annuity factor by $\bar{a}_{x}^{(\delta-\beta)} + k\bar{a}_{x/y}^{(\delta-\beta)}$, where y represents the age of the spouse at retirement. Again, this will lead to a reduction in the replacement rate. This contrasts with defined benefit schemes, where the survivor's pension is part of the benefit package. In a defined contribution scheme, a survivor's pension has to be traded off against a lower replacement rate.

The replacement rate will increase if either $\gamma^{*} - \delta$ decreases or $\delta - \beta$ increases. Thus a higher rate of interest relative to the rate of salary progression and/or of indexation increases the replacement rate.

4.5 THE EFFECT OF THE DENSITY FACTOR

The above discussion has assumed that the density of contributions is 100 per cent throughout the contributory career of the participant. If the density is uniform but less than 100 per cent, the accumulated balance and related entities, discussed in section 4.3 above, will be proportionately reduced.

If there are gaps in the contributory service, the density will vary over the contributory career of the member. In this section the effect of a single gap of m years during a total contributory career of n years is investigated.

Let the gap occur t years after the entry $(0 < t < n - m)$. The accumulated balance at the end of the career, assuming that the break in service does not affect the salary progression, will be given by

$$\pi \int_0^t e^{\gamma^* z} e^{\delta(n-z)} \, dz + \pi \int_{t+m}^n e^{\gamma^* z} e^{\delta(n-z)} \, dz = \pi \frac{e^{n\delta}}{\phi^*} [e^{\phi^* t}(1 - e^{\phi^* m}) - (1 - e^{\phi^* n})] \quad (4.8)$$

where $\phi^* = \gamma^* - \delta$. Differentiating the above expression with respect to t yields the following expression for the differential coefficient:

$$\pi e^{n\delta} e^{\phi^* t}(1 - e^{\phi^* m}) \quad (4.9)$$

It will be obvious that the differential coefficient is negative if $\gamma^* > \delta$ and positive otherwise. The following conclusions can be drawn:

- the location of the gap within the contributory career affects the balance;
- if the force of growth of the individual's salary exceeds the force of interest, the earlier the gap the higher the accumulated balance: otherwise, the later the gap the higher the balance.

The same conclusions are valid for the relative accumulated balance and other entities based on it.

On the other hand, in a defined benefit scheme in which the retirement pension is based on the final salary and is proportional to the contributory service period, the retirement pension, although affected by a gap in service, does not depend on the stage in the career where the gap occurs.

4.6 THE IMPORTANCE OF THE INTEREST ELEMENT

The discussion in sections 4.3 and 4.4 above has highlighted the importance of the interest element in the benefit derived from a defined contribution scheme. Of course, the interest element is equally important in a defined benefit scheme, but it intervenes in a different way; a higher interest yield on the reserves does not affect the benefits but will reduce the contributions which would otherwise be required under a financial system which involves a degree of funding. In a defined contribution scheme, on the other hand, the interest credited to individual balances in any period would be directly related to the yield on the invested funds of the scheme in the same period, which therefore has a direct effect on each individual's benefit. This suggests that both defined contribution and funded defined benefit schemes should aim at maximizing the yield on the invested reserves. It is not proposed here to enter into a discussion of the investment aspects of reserve funds, but it is noted that there are special considerations which arise with defined contribution schemes, in particular the need to engender confidence that the capital is reasonably protected (Daykin, 1996).

4.7 THE CONTRIBUTION RATE FOR A SPECIFIED REPLACEMENT RATE

For a person entering at age b and retiring at age r, the contribution rate which will lead to a pension computed at 1 per cent of the final salary per year of service can be established by equating the accumulated balance (4.1) to the value of the pension (payable for life) at retirement. This will give the following formula, which allows for indexation of the pension with force β:

$$
\pi = \frac{r-b}{100} e^{(r-b)(\gamma^* - \delta)} \frac{\bar{a}_r^{p(\delta - \beta)}}{\bar{a}\frac{(\delta - \gamma^*)}{r-b|}}
\tag{4.10}
$$

This may be compared with the expression (2.13) of Chapter 2, adapted in terms of the parameter γ^*:

$$
\pi = \frac{r-b}{100} \frac{D_r^{a(\delta - \gamma^*)}}{\bar{N}_b^{a(\delta - \gamma^*)}} \bar{a}_r^{p(\delta - \beta)}
\tag{4.11}
$$

The difference is that in (4.10) the equivalence is established at retirement age r, whereas in (4.11) it is established at entry age b. The expression (4.11) allows for decrements due to death or invalidity before retirement age, which means that the premium computed by (4.11) will be lower than that corresponding to (4.10). It is important to appreciate this difference and to note that the premium given by the simpler formula (4.10) is not an actuarial premium based on the insurance approach (Ferrara and Drouin, 1996).

4.8 TRANSFORMATION FROM DEFINED CONTRIBUTION TO DEFINED BENEFIT OR VICE VERSA

There is substantial difference of opinion among experts in regard to the relative advantages and disadvantages of defined contribution and defined benefit schemes (World Bank, 1994: Beattie and McGillivray, 1995). A compromise solution would consist in having both types of scheme simultaneously, in complementary tiers (Iyer, 1993). A social security pension reform could therefore involve the transformation, either partly or fully, of an existing scheme in either direction. The financial implications of such transformations are discussed below.

If a defined contribution scheme is to be transformed into a defined benefit scheme, an important question concerns the disposition of the accumulated balances of the members existing on the date of change. The possible options include (McGillivray, 1992, pp. 51–54):

(a) paying out the accumulated balances immediately;

(b) freezing the balances and paying them out, with the continued addition of interest, as and when due under the rules of the old scheme;

(c) converting the balances into annuities on the date of transformation;

(d) converting the accumulated balances into pension credits.

Option (d) is generally preferred owing particularly to the advantage that it will permit the defined benefit scheme to "take off" right from the outset. Members could be given the option to convert only a part of their balance into credits and to receive the remainder under old rules.

The following is a simple formula for converting accumulated balances into periods of service for the purpose of the defined benefit scheme. For example, if BAL represents the accumulated balance, SAL the salary on the date of conversion, and CR the contribution rate under the defined contribution scheme, the credited service period CDT could be taken as

$$\text{CDT} = \frac{\text{BAL}}{\text{SAL} \times \text{CR}} \tag{4.12}$$

This formula estimates the past service exactly if throughout membership the rate of interest credited to the balance was equal to the rate of increase of the contributory salary, and the contribution rate under the defined contribution scheme had remained unchanged. Otherwise, the formula should be adjusted. The additional pension earned by virtue of CDT would, in general, differ from the periodic payment resulting from converting BAL into an annuity according to the approach in section 4.4, above.

In the opposite case, when a partially funded defined benefit scheme is transformed into a fully funded defined contribution scheme, there will arise an unfunded accrued liability in respect of the past service of existing insured persons at the time of transformation, owing to the under-funding of service benefits under the defined benefit scheme. This is similar to the situation at the outset of an occupational pension scheme, as discussed in Chapter 2. The amortization of this liability would require special additional contributions, or in a social security scheme the government may assume the liability for past service. Since such a transformation normally requires the transition generation to bear a double burden (that is, payment of pensions to existing retired persons as well as contributions to their own individual accounts), the latter alternative is usually followed.

TECHNIQUES

THE PROJECTION TECHNIQUE FOR ACTUARIAL VALUATIONS

5

5.1 INTRODUCTION

Part II of this book is concerned with the practical aspects of the actuarial management of social security pension schemes. This chapter deals with the projection technique, which corresponds to the first of the two approaches for the analysis of pension schemes, mentioned in section 3.2 of Chapter 3. The present value technique, which corresponds to the second approach, is the subject of Chapter 6.

It is not the purpose of this chapter to produce a computer programme which can be readily applied to establish projections. Rather, the purpose is to elaborate on the basis and the methodology of the projection technique. Although invalidity and survivors' pensions are included in the treatment, the illustrations refer, as in Part I, mainly to retirement pensions and to a simple pension formula, directly related to the service period and the final salary.

5.2 ACTUARIAL VALUATIONS OF SOCIAL SECURITY PENSION SCHEMES

In Chapter 1, the theory of financing social security pension schemes was developed on the assumption that the projections made at the outset of the scheme would be exactly realized. However, this is highly unlikely, and in practice the experience will diverge from the projected values. In the first place, the actual values of the determining parameters – see section 1.2 – may differ from those assumed at the outset and, secondly, there will be stochastic variations around these parameters. Moreover, the scope of application of the scheme or the benefit provisions might have been modified in the interim. As a result, whatever the financial system adopted at the outset, as the experience unfolds there will be actuarial gains or losses, the cumulative effect of which will be reflected in the accumulated reserve fund.

There is also the question of the value placed on the reserve fund itself, because the fund will not in general be merely placed in a bank account at interest, but might be invested in a variety of assets (bonds, shares, real estate, and so on). Further, there are different approaches to the valuation of such assets (book value, market value, discounted value of future proceeds, and so on). Thus, it should be expected that at the time $t = n$, the actuarial valuation date, the reserve fund will diverge from the projected value which was designated as $V(n)$ in Chapter 1. To highlight this, the value placed on the reserve fund will be denoted by $Fd(n)$ in this chapter.

A second aspect concerns the parametric assumptions relating to the future. The assumptions made at the preceding actuarial valuation – at $t = n$ – for the period (n, m) may not be considered appropriate at $t = m$, on the basis of the analysis of the inter-valuation experience. The necessary modifications to the financing arrangements will need to be effected through an actuarial valuation of the scheme undertaken at $t = m$, based on revised assumptions in regard to the parameters and taking credit for the accumulated reserve fund, valued at $Fd(m)$.

Actuarial valuations of social security pension schemes are generally statutory requirements at prescribed intervals (three to five years). In addition, interim internal valuations may sometimes be performed. In view of the open fund approach and the application of partial funding, the projection technique is the appropriate technique for the valuation of social security pension schemes. The main purpose of a periodic valuation of an ongoing scheme is to test its long-term solvency, that is, to assess whether under the existing financing arrangements benefits can be paid and reserve funds maintained at the required levels. In this regard, particular importance attaches to changes in income and expenditure projections in successive valuations, which may signal the need to change the financing arrangements. Any significant proposed scheme modifications will require actuarial assessment through an ad hoc valuation. When performing an initial valuation preceding a scheme's introduction, computation for alternative financial systems will be required. In view of the uncertainty of future assumptions, sensitivity testing on the basis of multiple projections is indicated (McGillivray, 1996; Picard, 1996).

5.3   ALTERNATIVE PROJECTION METHODOLOGIES

There are different methodologies for social security pension scheme projections. These include (Crescentini and Spandonaro, 1992):

(a)   actuarial methods;

(b)   econometric methods; and

(c)   mixed methods.

Methods classified under (a) have long been applied in the field of insurance and have also proved valuable for social security projections. Methods classified under (b) are in effect extrapolations of past trends, using regression techniques. Essentially, the difference between the two is that actuarial methods depend on endogenous (that is, internal to the model) factors, whereas econometric methods are based on exogenous factors. Methods classified under (c) rely partly on endogenous and partly on exogenous factors. This chapter is mainly concerned with methods classified under (a) above, and to some extent with those classified under (c).

An approach which may be taken, when a substantial part of the population is covered and the scheme is fairly mature, is to use national population or labour force projections as the basis and apply appropriate proportions to the results of the national projections to derive social security projections. In this chapter a more general method of pension scheme projection, termed the component method, is described. However, this does not preclude reference to national population or labour force projections for determining certain projection factors or elements.

The *component method*, as the name suggests, breaks the covered population down into components and simulates the evolution of each component over time. The extent of the breakdown will depend on the availability of data for the valuation and also on the computing capacity at the disposal of the actuary. The minimum breakdown required is by category of covered person (i.e. active insured persons, retirees, invalids, widows/widowers and orphans), by male and female within each category and by single age within each sex. Additional breakdowns may include the analysis of the active population by past service and by income level. In this regard, it is evident that an additional breakdown can be justified only if it can be expected to lead to a commensurate increase in the precision of the projections.

In addition to the initial data, the inputs include assumptions on the parameters – such as those mentioned in section 1.2 – which will affect the evolution of the various components of the concerned aggregates. The methodology will need to be tailored to the level of complexity of the assumptions. In other words, depending on the nature of the assumptions, the methodology can sometimes be simplified – as indicated, for example, in section 5.13, below. This suggests that, generally speaking, the parametric assumptions should be kept as simple as possible, unless there are adequate grounds to do otherwise.

This chapter discusses alternative methodologies for the component method, which depend, on the one hand, on the nature of the available data and, on the other, on the nature of the assumptions in regard to the determining parameters.

5.4 DEMOGRAPHIC PROJECTIONS: GENERAL DESCRIPTION

The first step in the projection technique is the production of estimates of numbers of individuals in each of the principal population subgroups (active insured persons, retirees, invalids, widows/widowers, orphans) at discrete time-points $(t = 1, 2, \ldots)$, starting from given initial values (at $t = 0$).

The demographic projection procedure can be regarded as the iteration of a matrix multiplication operation, typified as follows (based on Crescentini and Spandonaro, 1992):

$$n_t = n_{t-1} Q_{t-1} \qquad (5.1)$$

in which n_t is a row vector whose elements represent the demographic projection values at time t and Q_{t-1} is a square matrix of transition probabilities for the interval $(t - 1, t)$, which take the form:

$$n_t = [A(t) \quad R(t) \quad I(t) \quad W(t) \quad O(t)]$$

$$Q_t = \begin{bmatrix} p^{(aa)} & q^{(ar)} & q^{(ai)} & q^{(aw)} & q^{(ao)} \\ 0 & p^{(rr)} & 0 & q^{(rw)} & q^{(ro)} \\ 0 & 0 & p^{(ii)} & q^{(iw)} & q^{(io)} \\ 0 & 0 & 0 & p^{(ww)} & 0 \\ 0 & 0 & 0 & 0 & p^{(oo)} \end{bmatrix}$$

The elements of the matrix and the symbols have the following significance:

$p^{(rr)}$ denotes the probability of remaining in the same status r;
$q^{(rs)}$ denotes the probability of transition from status r to status s;
a, r, i, w, and o respectively represent active lives, retirees, invalids, widows/widowers and orphans.

The above procedure, however, is not applied at the level of total numbers in the subpopulations. In order to improve precision, each subpopulation is sub-divided at least by sex and age. Preferably, the active population would be further subdivided by past service. The procedure is applied at the lowest level of subdivision and the results aggregated to give various subtotals and totals. The matrix Q will be sex–age specific; it can also be varied over time if required. *As regards survivors, an additional procedure is required after each iteration to classify new widows/widowers and orphans arising from the deaths of males/females aged x according to the age of the widow/widower (y) or of the orphan (z) before proceeding to the next iteration.*

5.5   DATA FOR DEMOGRAPHIC PROJECTIONS

For the initial covered pppulation, data on the date of valuation giving the sex–age breakdown of each of the subpopulations (active persons, retirees, inva-lids, widows/widowers and orphans) will provide the starting-point for the itera-tion procedure. As regards active persons on the valuation date, a distribution by past service within each sex–age group is desirable, if this can be expected to improve significantly the precision of the projections. It might be possible to adopt an ad hoc distribution of the active population around the average past service if, for example, the variance of the distribution can be estimated or assumed.

A practical problem concerns variations in the definition of "age". The possibilities include age last birthday, age nearest birthday and age next birthday. In this chapter, the procedures correspond to the definition *age nearest birthday*. This is for illustrative purposes only, and does not preclude the adoption of other age definitions which may be more suitable or convenient depending on the circumstances. Data provided according to any of the other definitions may be converted, by interpolation, to correspond to the definition adopted in this chapter; alternatively, the projection formulae could be adapted to suit the specific age definition of the data.

A second question concerns the reference period for the data. Generally an actuarial valuation is carried out as at the end of a financial year of the scheme. In this chapter, it is assumed that the data concerning beneficiaries relate to those in receipt of a pension on the valuation date, whereas the data concerning active insured persons relate to those who were credited with at least one contribution in the financial year preceding the valuation date. Either data set is assumed to be classified according to the nearest age on the valuation date.

With regard to future entrants into the scheme, it would be unusual to be able to make assumptions concerning their actual numbers by sex and age. Two variants are considered:

Variant (a): (based on ILO-PENS, 1997): The expected total active insured population – by sex and age – in future years is provided exogenously, that is, based on national population or labour force projections.

Variant (b): Indications are provided of the expected rate of growth of the total active insured population in each projection year, together with the *relative sex–age* distribution of the corresponding new entrants; often, the same sex–age distribution is assumed for all new entrant generations.

In either case, the actual new entrants of each projection year, by sex and age, would be deduced indirectly. New entrants are assumed to enter at the middle of the financial year. For consistency with the age definition adopted in this chapter for the valuation data (age nearest birthday), new entrants are classified by *age next birthday* at entry.

5.6 THE ACTUARIAL BASIS FOR DEMOGRAPHIC PROJECTIONS

For carrying out the demographic projections it is necessary to adopt a basis, consisting of the elements listed below. They should be understood to be sex specific. For brevity, time is not indicated as a variable, but some or all of *the bases may be varied over time.*

(a)   The active service table $\{l_x^a\}$, $b \le x \le r$, where b is the youngest entry age and r the highest retirement age. This is a double decrement table allowing for the decrements of death and invalidity only. The associated dependent rates of decrement are denoted by ${}^*q_x^a$ (mortality) and ${}^*i_x$ (invalidity). Retirement is assumed to take place at exact integral ages, just before each birthday, r_x denoting the proportion retiring at age x.

(b)   The life table for invalids $\{l_x^i\}$, $b \le x < \omega$ and the associated independent mortality rate q_x^i.

(c)   The life table for retired persons, $\{l_x^p\}$, $r^* \le x < \omega$ (where r^* is the lowest retirement age), and the associated independent rate of mortality q_x^p.

(d)   The double decrement table for widows/widowers, $\{l_y^w\}$, $y^* \le y < \omega$ (y^* is the lowest age of a widow/widower), and the associated dependent rates of decrement, ${}^*q_y^w$ (mortality) and ${}^*h_y$ (remarriage).

(e)   The single decrement table for orphans, $\{l_z^o\}$, $0 \le z \le z^*$, where z^* is the age limit for orphans' pensions and the associated independent rate of decrement q_z^o.

(f) w_x, the proportion of married persons among those dying at age x.

(g) y_x, the average age of the spouse of a person dying at age x.

(h) n_x, the average number of orphans of a person dying at age x.

(i) z_x, the average age of the above orphans.

(j) $\rho(t)$, the growth rate for the number of active insured persons in projection year t. **This applies to variant (b) of section 5.5 only.**

With regard to widows/widowers and orphans, it will be noted that average ages – corresponding to a given age x of the insured person – have been indicated. This does not exclude recourse to age distributions of widows/widowers and orphans, for increased precision (Boye, 1971; Picard, 1971). Further, the proportions and average ages indicated at (f), (g), (h) and (i) are taken as applicable to all categories of deceased – active person, invalid or retiree – but could be varied by category.

5.7   EXPRESSIONS FOR TRANSITION PROBABILITIES

The following expressions for the age- (and sex-) specific one-year transition probabilities are based on the rules of addition and multiplication of probabilities. They are consistent with international practice (based on Picard, 1975).

Each iteration is assumed to operate immediately *after* the retirements (occurring at the end of each year of age) have taken place. Under the assumption of uniform distribution of decrements over each year of age, the decrements affecting active persons, retirees and existing invalids – in (5.4), (5.5a), (5.7) and (5.9) – are assumed to occur, on average, at the end of six months; new invalids dying before the end of the year are assumed to die at the end of nine months (in (5.5b)).

Active to active

$$p_x^{(aa)} = (1 - {}^*q_x^a - {}^*i_x)(1 - r_{x+1})$$ (5.2)

Active to retiree

$$q_x^{(ar)} = (1 - {}^*q_x^a - {}^*i_x)r_{x+1}$$ (5.3)

Active to invalid

$$q_x^{(ai)} = {}^*i_x(1 - 0.5q_x^i)$$ (5.4)

Active to widow/widower

$$q_x^{(aw)} = q_x^{(aw1)} + q_x^{(aw2)}$$ (5.5)

$$q_x^{(aw1)} = {}^*q_x^a w_{x+0.5}[1 - 0.5({}^*q_{y_x}^w + {}^*h_{y_x})]$$ (5.5a)

$$q_x^{(aw2)} = {}^*i_x \tfrac{1}{2}q_x^i w_{x+0.75}[1 - 0.25({}^*q_{y_x}^w + {}^*h_{y_x})]$$ (5.5b)

Retiree to retiree

$$p_x^{(rr)} = 1 - q_x^p$$ (5.6)

Retiree to widow/widower

$$q_x^{(rw)} = q_x^p w_{x+0.5}[1 - 0.5({}^*q_{y_x}^w + {}^*h_{y_x})]$$ (5.7)

Invalid to invalid

$$p_x^{(ii)} = 1 - q_x^i$$ (5.8)

Invalid to widow/widower

$$q_x^{(iw)} = q_x^i w_{x+0.5}[1 - 0.5({}^*q_{y_x}^w + {}^*h_{y_x})]$$ (5.9)

Widow/widower to widow/widower

$$p_x^{(ww)} = 1 - {}^*q_x^w - {}^*h_x$$ (5.10)

It will be noted that equation (5.5) has two components: (5.5a) relating to deaths of active insured persons in the age range $(x, x+1)$; and (5.5b) relating to active persons becoming invalid and then dying by age $x + 1$. It is understood that the values of w_x corresponding to fractional ages which occur in the above formulae would be obtained by interpolation between the values at adjacent integral ages. Expressions for transition probabilities concerning orphans, corresponding to (5.5a), (5.5b), (5.7), (5.9) and (5.10), can be derived on the same lines as for widows/widowers.

Remark: With regard to the survival factor after the transition of status – in (5.4), (5.5a), (5.5b), (5.7) and (5.9) – strictly speaking, a correction is required in order to be consistent with the assumption of the uniform distribution of decrements. For example, formula (5.4) assumes that the probability of death of an invalid, aged $x + t$, in the fractional interval $(x + t, x + 1)$ can be expressed as $(1 - t)q_x^i$. This implies, however, that in the interval $(x, x + 1)$,

$$\frac{1}{l_{x+t}^i} = \frac{1-t}{l_x^i} + \frac{t}{l_{x+1}^i}$$

which has the somewhat illogical consequence of a decreasing force of mortality in the interval. The more logical, linear, assumption

$$l_{x+t}^i = (1 - t)l_x^i + tl_{x+1}^i$$

would lead to the following result for the probability of death of an invalid, aged $x + t$, in $(x + t, x + 1)$:

$$\frac{(1 - t)q_x^i}{1 - tq_x^i}$$

Such a correction may be introduced, if desired, leading to the following expression for the transition probability:

$$q_x^{(ai)} = {}^*i_x\left(1 - \frac{0.5q_x^i}{1 - 0.5q_x^i}\right)$$

In practice the simpler expression (5.4) might, however, be adequate. This also applies to formulae (5.5a), (5.5b), (5.7) and (5.9).

5.8   THE DEMOGRAPHIC PROJECTION FORMULAE

Starting from the population data on the date of the valuation $(t = 0)$, provided as indicated in section 5.5 above, the transition probabilities are applied to successive projections by sex and age (and preferably by past service, in the case of the active population). In the case of the active population projection, new entrants of the immediately preceding year have to be incorporated before proceeding to the next iteration. The projection formulae for the active insured population are given below; the method of projecting the beneficiary populations is illustrated with reference to retirement pensioners.

Notation

- $Act(x, s, t)$ denotes the active population aged x *nearest birthday*, with *curtate* past service duration s years, at time t; $b \leq x < r, s \geq 0$.

- $Ac(x,t)$ denotes the active population aged x *nearest birthday* at time t. The corresponding beneficiary populations are denoted by $Re(x,t)$, $In(x,t)$ and $Wi(x,t)$.
- $A(t)$ denotes the total active population at time t. The corresponding beneficiary populations are denoted by $R(t)$, $I(t)$ and $W(t)$.
- The number of new entrants aged x *next birthday* in the projection year t, that is, in the interval $(t-1,t)$, is denoted by $N(x,t)$.

Active population projections: variant (a)

The projection of the active population from time $t-1$ to time t is expressed by the equation

$$Act(x,s,t) = Act(x-1,s-1,t-1)p^{(aa)}_{x-1} \qquad (5.11)$$

where $b+1 \le x < r$, $s \ge 1$. This assumes that the benefit density, that is, the proportion of the potential period of service in the age interval $(x-1,x)$ which is effectively reckoned for pension purposes – see (f) under section 5.11, below – is unity. More generally, if db denotes this benefit density,

$$Act(x,s,t) = [db\,Act(x-1,s-1,t-1) + (1-db)Act(x-1,s,t-1)]p^{(aa)}_{x-1} \qquad (5.12)$$

In this variant, $Ac(x,t)$ will be given exogenously. The active survivors, at time t, of the new entrants during the year $(t-1,t)$ will then be given by

$$Z(x,t) = Ac(x,t) - \sum_{s>0} Act(x,s,t) - (1-db)Act(x-1.0,t-1)p^{(aa)}_{x-1} \qquad (5.13)$$

where $b \le x < r$ and the summation extends from $s = 1$ to the upper limit of s. It will be noted that the last term in (5.13) will not occur if the density is unity and in that case $Act(x,0,t) = Z(x,t)$. Otherwise,

$$Act(x,0,t) = Z(x,t) + (1-db)Act(x-1,0,t-1)p^{(aa)}_{x-1} \qquad (5.14)$$

These new entrants are assumed to have entered at the middle of the year. The actual number of new entrants, *at age x next birthday*, can be estimated by reverse projection as

$$N(x,t) = \frac{Z(x,t)}{p^{(aa)}_{x-0.5:0.5}} \qquad (5.15)$$

The factor in the denominator is analogous to $p^{(aa)}_x$ but refers to the age interval $(x-0.5,x)$ and has the expression

$$p^{(aa)}_{x-0.5:0.5} = (1 - 0.5(^*q^a_{x-1} + {}^*i_{x-1}))(1 - r_x) \qquad (5.16)$$

Active population projections: variant (b)

$Act(x, s, t)$ for $b + 1 \leq x < r, s \geq 1$, is projected as in variant (a) – see (5.11) and (5.12).

In this variant, the rate of increase of the total active insured population, $\rho(t)$, is given. The total active population at time t is first projected by the formula

$$A(t) = A(t - 1)(1 + \rho(t)) \tag{5.17}$$

In this variant, the proportionate age distribution of new entrants by *age next birthday* at entry, $pr(x)$, is also given. $Z(x, t)$ is then estimated by the formula

$$Z(x, t) = \frac{A(t) - \sum_y \left(\sum_{s>0} Act(y, s, t) + (1 - db)Act(y - 1, 0, t - 1)p_{y-1}^{(aa)} \right)}{\sum_y pr(y)p_{y-0.5:0.5}^{(aa)}}$$
$$\times pr(x)p_{x-0.5:0.5}^{(aa)} \tag{5.18}$$

The summations in the numerator run respectively over the relevant age range and over $s \geq 1$. $Act(x, 0, t)$ and $N(x, t)$ are then computed as in variant (a) – see (5.14) and (5.15)..

Remark: In the above development, it has been assumed that $Z(x, t)$ is always positive. If negative results are obtained for $Z(x, t)$ and therefore for $N(x, t)$, this may be interpreted as signifying that there are no new entrants but that, on the other hand, $|N(x, t)|$ active insured persons withdrew from the active insured status. This would correspond to the situation where there is a significant *latent* covered population, possibly with deferred pension rights, not currently contributing but potentially able to revert to contributory status. The projection model can be adapted to this situation by treating this group as a distinct subpopulation and projecting it separately with assumed rates of re-entry into active contributory status. This is, however, not pursued further in this chapter.

Beneficiary population projections

The projection procedure for the various beneficiary populations is illustrated below with reference to retirement pensioners:

(a)   retired population aged x at time t:

$$Re(x, t) = Re(x - 1, t - 1)p_{x-1}^{(rr)} + Ac(x - 1, t - 1)q_{x-1}^{(ar)} + N(x, t)q_{x-0.5:0.5}^{(ar)} \tag{5.19}$$

where the last projection factor is analogous to $q_x^{(ar)}$ but relates to the age range $(x - 0.5, x)$ and has the expression

$$q_{x-0.5:0.5}^{(ar)} = (1 - 0.5(^*q_{x-1}^a + {^*i_{x-1}}))r_x \tag{5.20}$$

(b)   total retired population

$$R(t) = \sum_x Re(x, t) \tag{5.21}$$

where $x \geq b$ and the summation extends from $b + 1$ to ω.

Remark: It has been implicitly assumed that all new retirees, the second and third elements of $Re(x, t)$ – see (5.19) – are entitled to retirement pensions. If a qualifying condition – in terms of a minimum service period – applies, the second element should be analysed into its components, that is, expressed as

$$\sum_s Act(x - 1, s - 1, t - 1)q_{x-1}^{(ar)}$$

and only those components included which would qualify for pension. Similarly, the third element of $Re(x, t)$, which would have only half-a-year or less of service, would be excluded under the operation of qualifying conditions, if applicable. This remark is equally valid for the projections of invalidity and widows'/widowers' pensions.

5.9   FINANCIAL PROJECTIONS: GENERAL DESCRIPTION

After the demographic projections – as described in section 5.4, above – are completed, the next step is the production of estimates of the total annual insured salary bill and of the total annual amounts of the different categories of pensions "in force" at discrete time points $(t = 1, 2, \ldots)$ starting from given initial values at $t = 0$. These aggregates are obtained by applying the appropriate per capita average amounts (of salaries or of pensions, as the case may be) to each individual element of the demographic projections and then summing. The average amounts are computed year by year in parallel with the progress of the corresponding demographic projection. An average per capita amount (salary or pension, as the case may be) is computed for each distinct population element generated by the demographic projection; if different elements are aggregated in the demographic projection – for example, existing invalids surviving from age x to $x + 1$ and new invalids reaching age $x + 1$ at the same time – a weighted per capita average amount is computed to correspond to the aggregated population element.

Two different methods will be described below in regard to the projection of the insured salary.

Method 1: The first method, which is classical, refers to age- and time-related average salaries which are projected, allowing for the progression of each cohort's average salary according to an age-related salary scale function and taking into account the escalation of the general level of salaries, but the method assumes an invariant salary scale function. Although the starting salaries of new entrant cohorts could be varied, this method does not permit the adequate modelling of the variation over time in the age-wise salary structure of the active population. Nor does it allow the salary distribution at each age to be taken into account.

Method 2 (based on ILO-DIST, 1996): This method begins by modelling a variation over time in the age-related average salary structure, and then computes age- and time-related average salaries allowing for general salary escalation. Further, it models the salary distribution by age, which can increase the precision of the financial projections.

5.10   DATA FOR FINANCIAL PROJECTIONS

For the initial active population, the starting data will consist of the sex-specific average insured salary at each age x, denoted by $s(x, 0)$. It is assumed that the salaries relate to the annual rates of salary "in force" on the date of the valuation, that is, the potential salary corresponding to full-time work over one whole year.

In addition, for the application of *method 2* a salary distribution at each age of the initial population would be required. Alternatively, an indication of the *coefficient of variation* of this distribution – denoted by $cv(x)$ – should be provided.

The salary may refer to the total salary, or to the salary relevant to the social security pension scheme, that is, the salary subject to a specified threshold and/ or ceiling. In the former case, a "catchment factor" should be applied to derive the relevant salary. It is assumed in this chapter that the reference is to the total salary.

For pensioners existing on the valuation date, sex-specific average annual pension amounts "in force" at each age and for each category of pensioner will be required.

Another datum for the financial analysis is the accumulated reserve fund on the valuation date, denoted by $Fd(0)$.

5.11   THE ACTUARIAL BASIS FOR FINANCIAL PROJECTIONS

The basis for the financial projections would comprise assumptions in regard to the following elements. They are specified as functions of age or time; the age-related elements should be understood to be sex specific and *may be further varied over time*, if necessary.

(a)   For *method 1*: the age-related salary scale function: s_x.

   For *method 2*: The factor indicating the change in the age-wise average salary structure $j(t)$.

(b)   The rate of salary escalation in each projection year: $\gamma(t)$.

(c)   The rate of pension indexation in each projection year: $\beta(t)$.

(d) The rate of investment return in each projection year: $i(t)$.

(e) The contribution density, that is, the fraction of the year during which contributions are effectively payable, $dc(x)$.

(f) The benefit density, that is, the fraction of the potential period of service which will effectively be reckoned for pension purposes, $db(x)$ – which may exceed $dc(x)$ due to crediting of non-contributory periods.

5.12 THE FINANCIAL PROJECTION FORMULAE

Projection of average salaries: Method 1

The basic formula for the projection of the average salary of any cohort, aged x in year t, starting from the average salary a year earlier, is

$$Sal(x,t) = s(x-1,t-1)\frac{s_x}{s_{x-1}}(1+\gamma(t)) \tag{5.22}$$

$s(x,t)$, which denotes the average salary of the whole active population aged x *nearest birthday* at time t, would be obtained by taking the weighted average of the salary of the cohort surviving from $t-1$ and that of the new entrant cohort entering in the year $(t-1,t)$, assumed to enter at age x *next birthday* at the middle of the year. For the latter group, the average salary at the end of the year of entry, denoted by $sn(x,t)$, is taken as

$$sn(x,t) = s(x-0.5,0)[\pi_1'(1+\gamma(z))]\frac{s_x}{s_{x-0.5}} \tag{5.23}$$

Projection of average salaries: Method 2

The initial *relative salary function*, denoted by $ss(x,0)$, which indicates the relative levels of age-wise average salaries at $t=0$, is established by expressing the average salary at age x as an index – with, say, 1,000 at the youngest age b – as follows:

$$ss(x,0) = 1000\frac{s(x,0)}{s(b,0)} \tag{5.24}$$

The relative salary function for projection year t is then computed by the formula

$$ss(x,t) = ss(x-1,t)\left[\frac{ss(x,0)}{ss(x-1,0)}\right]^{j(t)} \tag{5.25}$$

It will be noted that a value of the adjustment factor $j(t)$ greater/smaller than unity implies a widening/narrowing of the variation of the average salary by age. If $j(t)=0$, the average salary becomes the same at all ages.

The average salary at age x in projection year t is then computed by the formula

$$s(x,t) = ss(x,t)(1+\gamma(t))\frac{\sum_b^{r-1} s(y,t-1)Ac(y,t-1)}{\sum_b^{r-1} ss(y,t)Ac(y,t)} \frac{\sum_b^{r-1} Ac(y,t)}{\sum_b^{r-1} Ac(y,t-1)} \qquad (5.26)$$

where $Ac(y,t)$ denotes the projected active population aged y at time t.

The total insured salary bill "in force" at time t would be estimated as $\sum_x Ac(x,t)s(x,t)dc(x)$. As mentioned in section 5.10 above, a "catchment factor" should be applied if $s(x,t)$ refers to the total salary and not to the insured salary.

Projection of salary distributions

Depending on the pension formula, the precision of the benefit expenditure projections can be improved by using salary distributions.

The salary distribution at any age x is assumed to be *lognormal* (ILO-DIST, 1996). This means that the natural logarithm of the salary is normally distributed. Let y denote the salary and let $z = \log_e y$. Let μ_y and μ_z denote the respective means and σ_y^2 and σ_z^2 the respective variances. These parameters are connected by the relationships

$$\mu_y = e^{\mu_z + \frac{1}{2}\sigma_z^2} \qquad (5.27)$$

$$\sigma_y^2 = e^{2\mu_z + \sigma_z^2}(e^{\sigma_z^2} - 1) \qquad (5.28)$$

The average salary having been already projected, $\mu_y = s(x,t)$. If the *coefficient of variation* of y is assumed to be invariant at the initial value $cv(x)$, then $\sigma_y = cv(x)s(x,t)$. The parameters of the distribution of z can then be computed as follows by reversing the above formulae:

$$\mu_z = \log_e\left(\frac{\mu_y}{\sqrt{1+cv(x)^2}}\right) \qquad (5.29)$$

$$\sigma_z^2 = \log_e(1+cv(x)^2) \qquad (5.30)$$

It can be shown (see Appendix 6) that the average salary of the population between any two salary levels, say y_a and y_b, is given by

$$s(x,t)\frac{\Phi(w_b - \sigma_z) - \Phi(w_a - \sigma_z)}{\Phi(w_b) - \Phi(w_a)} \qquad (5.31)$$

where $\Phi(w)$ is the distribution function of the standard normal variate, $w_a = (\log_e y_a - \mu_z)/\sigma_z$ and $w_b = (\log_e y_b - \mu_z)/\sigma_z$.

In practice, the active population at each age, $Ac(x,t)$, would be partitioned into a limited number of groups according to salary level. For example, three groups may be used:

(a) the low income group (the lowest 30 per cent of the population);

(b) the middle income group (the middle 40 per cent);

(c) the high income group (the highest 30 per cent);

Let $s1(x,t)$, $s2(x,t)$ and $s3(x,t)$ denote the respective average salaries. First, the values w_1 and w_2 are determined such that $\Phi(w_1) = 0.3$ and $\Phi(w_2) = 0.7$. The average salaries are then given by

$$s1(x,t) = s(x,t)\frac{\Phi(w_1 - \sigma_z)}{\Phi(w_1)} \qquad (5.32)$$

$$s2(x,t) = s(x,t)\frac{\Phi(w_2 - \sigma_z) - \Phi(w_1 - \sigma_z)}{\Phi(w_2) - \Phi(w_1)} \qquad (5.33)$$

$$s3(x,t) = s(x,t)\frac{1 - \Phi(w_2 - \sigma_z)}{1 - \Phi(w_2)} \qquad (5.34)$$

Projection of benefit expenditure

As explained in section 5.9, an average per capita pension amount should be determined for each distinct beneficiary population element in the corresponding demographic projections. A weighted average per capita pension amount is then computed for those elements which are amalgamated at any particular stage in the projection process. This is illustrated below with reference to retirement pensions.

Let $b(x,t)$ denote the average per capita pension amount of the $Re(x,t)$ retirement pensioners aged x at time t. From equation (5.19), it is seen that $Re(x,t)$ is constituted by amalgamating three distinct elements. The per capita pension amount appropriate to each element should therefore be determined and a weighted average then taken.

The per capita pension amount of the first element would be determined as

$$b(x,t) = b(x - 1, t - 1)(1 + \beta(t)) \qquad (5.35)$$

The second element of $Re(x,t)$ relates to those retiring out of the active population aged $x - 1$ one year earlier, that is, $Ac(x - 1, t - 1)$. The simplest case is where a distribution by past service is not used but computations are based on the average past service of cohorts. Let the average contributory service of the $Ac(x - 1, t - 1)$ persons be denoted by $sv(x - 1, t - 1)$. The service after one year of this group would be projected as

$$sv(x,t) = sv(x - 1, t - 1) + db(x - 0.5) \qquad (5.36)$$

Under the assumptions made, the retirements take place at the end of each year of age. If the pension is based on the salary at retirement, and *method 1* applies, the reference salary would be $Sal(x,t)$ – see (5.22). If, for example, the pension formula is 1 per cent of the final salary per year of service, the pension amount per head would be given by

$$\frac{sv(x,t)}{100} Sal(x,t) \tag{5.37}$$

If **method 2** applies, the second element of $Re(x,t)$ would be regarded as being constituted of three subgroups with average salaries $s1(x,t)$, $s2(x,t)$ and $s3(x,t)$ – see (5.32), (5.33) and (5.34); the pension amount would then be computed for each subgroup, and a weighted average taken. If, in addition, a distribution by past service is available, $Ac(x,t)$ would be regarded as constituted by first-level subgroups $Act(x,s,t)$ – see (5.11) – according to past service s, each first-level subgroup being constituted by three second-level subgroups according to the level of the salary. (This ignores the correlation between salary level and past service, if any, but ad hoc adjustments may be possible in specific instances.) A per capita pension amount would be computed for each second-level subgroup and then a weighted average taken over all second-level subgroups. Such detailed analysis may not be justified in the case of a simple pension formula such as the one in (5.37), but if the formula is more complex – involving minimum or maximum percentage rates or varying rates of accrual, or being subject to minimum or maximum amounts – such analysis could significantly improve the precision of the projections and would therefore be justified.

The third element of $Re(x,t)$ corresponds to retirements arising out of the new entrants of the immediately preceding year $(t-1,t)$. This group would have a past service of half-a-year or less. The salary will be taken as $sn(x,t)$ under method 1 – see (5.23) – and as identical to that of the second element under method 2.

It is understood that if the various projected average salaries refer to the total salary, appropriate "catchment factors" should be applied at each stage to estimate the corresponding average insured salaries.

5.13 AN ALTERNATIVE PROJECTION METHOD UNDER SIMPLIFIED ASSUMPTIONS

In certain circumstances, it will be sufficient to produce projections for a single generation of new entrants from which the combined result for all new entrant generations can be obtained by a process known as *binding*. This is then combined with a separate closed-fund projection relating to the initial population, to obtain the required open-fund projections.

Demographic projections

The projection exercise pertaining to a typical generation of new entrants might relate, without loss of generality, to a standard population of 100,000 new entrants assumed to enter on the valuation date. Let the projected total active population at duration z be denoted by $IA(z)$ for the initial population projections and by $NA(z)$ for the standard projection of the new entrant generation. Given the rate of increase of the active population in each projection year $\rho(z)$, the actual number of new entrants, $na(z)$, assumed to enter at the middle of the year, is deduced by equating two different expressions for the active population at the end of projection year t (Picard, 1979):

$$IA(0) \prod_{z=1}^{t} (1 + \rho(z)) = IA(t) + \sum_{z=1}^{t} \frac{na(z)}{100,000} NA(t - z + 0.5) \qquad (5.38)$$

If the projection period is n years, there will be n such equations $(t = 1, 2, \ldots, n)$ which can be solved successively for the numbers $na(t)$. For example, the number of new entrants in the first projection year is given by

$$na(1) = \frac{IA(0)(1 + \rho(1)) - IA(1)}{NA(0.5)} 100,000 \qquad (5.39)$$

In (5.38), the value of $NA(t - z + 0.5)$ would be obtained by interpolation between $NA(t - z)$ and $NA(t - z + 1)$. After solving for $na(z)$, $z = 1, 2, \ldots, n$, these values will be used to derive the projections of the beneficiaries of various types of pensions. For example, if $IR(z)$ denotes the number of pensioners at duration z in the initial population projection and $NR(z)$ denotes the corresponding number resulting from the standard projection of 100,000 new entrants, the total number of pensioners at the end of the tth year of projection deriving from the initial population, as well as from the new entrants of the first t years, is given by

$$TR(t) = IR(t) + \sum_{z=1}^{t} \frac{na(z)}{100,000} NR(t - z + 0.5) \qquad (5.40)$$

In (5.40), the first component on the right-hand side represents the pensioners arising from the initial population, while the second member represents the pensioners arising from new entrants entering during the first t years, both as at the end of the tth year of projection.

Financial projections

Let the projections of total salaries for the initial population and for the standard generation of new entrants be denoted by $IS(t)$ and $NS(t)$ and the projections of total pensions by $IP(t)$ and $NP(t)$.

The total insured salaries at the end of the tth year of projection deriving from the initial population and from the new entrants of the first t years is given by

$$TS(t) = IS(t) + \sum_{z=1}^{t} \frac{na(z)}{100,000} NS(t - z + 0.5) ADJ(z) \qquad (5.41)$$

where $ADJ(z)$ is an adjustment factor given by

$$ADJ(z) = \frac{\prod_{r=t-z+1}^{t}(1+\gamma(r))}{\sqrt{1+\gamma(t-z+1)}} \tag{5.42}$$

It will be noted that $ADJ(z)$ provides the additional salary escalation required to bring $NS(t-z+0.5)$ up to the general level of salaries as at the end of the tth projection year.

Under the condition that $(1+\gamma(z))$ bears a constant ratio – independent of z – to $(1+\beta(z))$, a similar formula can be used to estimate the total pensions at the end of the tth year of projection, using the same adjustment factors. Thus,

$$TP(t) = IP(t) + \sum_{z=1}^{t} \frac{na(z)}{100,000} NP(t-z+0.5)ADJ(z) \tag{5.43}$$

It should be noted that if the above condition is not satisfied, it will, in general, not be possible to apply a simple formula such as (5.43).

5.14 MANIPULATION OF FINANCIAL PROJECTIONS FOR VALUATION PURPOSES

Based on the given (initial) and the projected values of total annual insured salaries and of total annual amounts of pensions "in force" at the time points $t = 0,1,2,\ldots,n$, the respective aggregates for the projection years $1,2,\ldots,n$ would be obtained by a numerical integration method. A margin for costs of administration would be added to the projected benefit expenditures. Let the projected amounts of insured salaries and of total expenditure (including administration) for the tth projection year be denoted by S_t and B_t, $t = 1,2,\ldots,n$.

It is often useful to discount the above aggregates to the date of the valuation. The discounted values are denoted by DS_t and DB_t. For example,

$$DS_t = \frac{S_t}{\left[\prod_{r=1}^{t-1}(1+i(r))\right]\sqrt{(1+i(t))}} \tag{5.44}$$

The discounted values are then accumulated, starting with the first year, to yield the totals of discounted salaries and benefits, denoted by TDS_t and TDB_t. For example,

$$TDS_t = \sum_{r=1}^{t} DS_r \tag{5.45}$$

In valuations of ongoing schemes, the main interest would be in testing the adequacy of the existing financing arrangements. Typically, this will require testing whether a specified schedule of the contribution rates C_t for the n years following the valuation will lead to a pattern of accumulation of the reserve fund which will satisfy a predetermined criterion such as:

(a) exceed at the end of each financial year a given proportion of that year's pension expenditure; or

(b) satisfy a certain growth pattern (e.g. at no stage suffer negative growth).

To carry out the above test, it would first be necessary to project the growth of the reserve fund, denoted by $V(t)$, starting from the initial value, $Fd(0)$. This is accomplished by the repeated application of the following recurrence formula (for $t = 1, \ldots, n$):

$$V(t) = V(t-1)(1 + i(t)) + [C_t S_t - B_t]\sqrt{1 + i(t)} \qquad (5.46)$$

When carrying out an initial valuation, preceding the introduction of a pension scheme, alternative financial systems will need to be modelled. This would also apply to an ongoing scheme if a change in the existing financial arrangements is being considered. The computations are illustrated for selected financial systems, below.

For the pay-as-you-go system, the projected contribution rate for the tth financial year is given by

$$\text{PAYG}_t = \frac{B_t}{S_t} \qquad (5.47)$$

As regards the other financing methods for social security pension schemes discussed in Chapter 1, the continuous formulae developed in that chapter can be adapted to the discrete case by replacing the integrals

$$\int_n^m B(t)\,e^{-\delta t}\,dt \quad \text{and} \quad \int_n^m S(t)\,e^{-\delta t}\,dt$$

occurring in the formulae by $\text{TDB}_m - \text{TDB}_n$ and $\text{TDS}_m - \text{TDS}_n$ respectively. Further, the functions $B(m)\,e^{-\delta m}$ and $S(m)\,e^{-\delta m}$ which also appear in the formulae will be obtained by interpolation between the projected values for the mth and $m+1^{\text{th}}$ financial years. The procedure is illustrated for selected financial systems, below. The valuation date is taken as the origin of the time axis.

The general average premium – see formula (1.13) of Chapter 1 – can be computed provided the projections are continued until the time when financial maturity is reached. Suppose maturity is reached by the nth projection year. Let i^*, ρ^* and γ^* indicate the eventual (constant) values of the investment return, new entrant growth and salary escalation factors, where, for obvious reasons,

$$1 + i^* > (1 + \rho^*)(1 + \gamma^*)$$

and let

$$v = \frac{(1 + \rho^*)(1 + \gamma^*)}{(1 + i^*)}$$

The GAP, taking into account the reserve fund on valuation date $(t = 0)$, is then given by

$$\text{GAP} = \frac{\text{TDB}_{n-1} + k\text{DB}_n - Fd(0)}{\text{TDS}_{n-1} + k\text{DS}_n} \tag{5.48}$$

where $k = 1/(1 - v)$.

The scaled premium corresponding to an initial period of m years following the valuation date $(t = 0)$ – see formula (1.32) of Chapter 1 – can be computed as

$$\pi(0, m) = \frac{\sqrt{\text{DB}_m \text{DB}_{m+1}} + \delta_m \text{TDB}_m - \delta_m Fd(0)}{\sqrt{\text{DS}_m \text{DS}_{m+1}} + \delta_m \text{TDS}_m} \tag{5.49}$$

where the geometric interpolation method has been used.

δ_m may be approximated by

$$\delta_m = \log_e(1 + i(m)) \tag{5.50}$$

The accumulated reserve fund, at the end of the period, starting from the initial reserve of $Fd(0)$ – see formula (1.5) of Chapter 1 – will be given by

$$V(m) = [Fd(0) + \pi(0, m)\text{TDS}_m - \text{TDB}_m] \left[\prod_{r=1}^{m} (1 + i(r)) \right] \tag{5.51}$$

An alternative expression – based on formula (1.31) of Chapter 1 – is

$$V(m) = \frac{\sqrt{B_m B_{m+1}} - \pi(0, m)\sqrt{S_m S_{m+1}}}{\delta_m} \tag{5.52}$$

The interpolation has again been based on the geometric method.

The formulae pertaining to the other financial systems can be similarly adapted for the purposes of computation.

THE PRESENT VALUE TECHNIQUE

6

6.1 INTRODUCTION

This chapter deals with the second of the two techniques for the analysis of pension schemes. This technique considers one cohort of insured persons at a time and computes the probable present values of the future insured salaries, on the one hand, and of the pension benefits payable to the members of the cohort and to their survivors, on the other.

This technique is naturally suited to the valuation of occupational pension schemes, which, as was seen in Chapter 2, are generally fully funded. This is not the case with partially funded social security pension schemes, for which the projection technique is the appropriate valuation technique. Nevertheless, the present value technique can provide additional financial insight and can therefore be a useful adjunct to the projection technique. The present value technique has already been introduced in Chapter 2, but in its continuous form and as regards retirement pensions only. Equation (2.12) in fact represents the level contribution rate $K(b)$, resulting from equating, for a cohort entering at age b and retiring at age r, $K(b)$ times the probable present value of future salaries to the probable present value of future retirement pensions.

In what follows, discrete approximations to the continuous commutation functions will be developed, in order to permit practical application of the theory. The treatment will be extended to invalidity and survivors' benefits. Reference will be made to the same demographic and financial bases as for the projection technique, detailed in sections 5.6 and 5.11 of Chapter 5. However, certain simplifications in the bases are adopted. First, the variation over time of the economic bases will not be considered. Thus $\gamma(t)$, $\beta(t)$ and $\delta(t)$ are assumed constant, and "interest" rates i and j and corresponding discounting factors are introduced where

$$i = \frac{1+\delta}{1+\gamma} - 1; \qquad v = \frac{1}{1+i} \tag{6.1}$$

$$j = \frac{1+\delta}{1+\beta} - 1; \qquad u = \frac{1}{1+j} \tag{6.2}$$

Second, the density factors dc and db are taken as unity at all ages. Finally, only a single retirement age r will be modelled, b being the youngest entry age.

The present value formulae will be developed for the simple case where the pension (for retirement or invalidity) accrues at 1 per cent of the final salary per year of service. For a more general treatment, reference should be made to an actuarial textbook on occupational pensions (for example, Lee, 1986).

The surviving spouse's pension is denoted by a proportion RWP of the actual or potential pension of the deceased, and each orphan's pension by a proportion ROP of the deceased's pension.

6.2   SPECIAL COMMUTATION FUNCTIONS

A series of (sex-specific) special commutation functions are needed for applying the present value technique. These are based on one or other of the decrement tables mentioned in section 5.6, or on combinations of them. Functions based on the active service table will be computed at interest rate i, while those based on the other tables will be computed at rate j.

Functions based on the active service table ($b \leq x \leq r$)

$$D_x^a = l_x^a v^x \tag{6.3}$$

$$D_x^{as} = s_x D_x^a \tag{6.4}$$

$$\bar{D}_x^{as} = \frac{D_x^{as} + D_{x+1}^{as}}{2} \tag{6.5}$$

$$\bar{N}_x^{as} = \sum_{t=x}^{r-1} \bar{D}_t^{as} \tag{6.6}$$

Functions based on the life table for invalids ($b \leq x < \omega$)

$$D_x^i = l_x^i u^x \tag{6.7}$$

$$\bar{D}_x^i = \frac{D_x^i + D_{x+1}^i}{2} \tag{6.8}$$

$$\bar{N}_x^i = \sum_{t=x}^{\omega} \bar{D}_t^i \tag{6.9}$$

$$\bar{a}_x^i = \frac{\bar{N}_x^i}{D_x^i} \tag{6.10}$$

Functions based on the double decrement table for widows/widowers
$(y^* \le y < \omega)$

$$D_y^w = l_y^w u^y \tag{6.11}$$

$$\bar{D}_y^w = \frac{D_y^w + D_{y+1}^w}{2} \tag{6.12}$$

$$\bar{N}_y^w = \sum_{t=y}^{\omega} \bar{D}_y^w \tag{6.13}$$

$$\bar{a}_y^w = \frac{\bar{N}_y^w}{D_y^w} \tag{6.14}$$

Functions based on the active service table and the life table for invalids
$(b \le x < r)$

$$C_x^{ai} = D_x^a * i_x v^{0.5} \bar{a}_{x+0.5}^i \tag{6.15}$$

$$C_x^{ais} = s_{x+0.5} C_x^{ai} \tag{6.16}$$

Functions based on the active service table and the decrement table for widows/widowers $(b \le x < r)$

$$G_{x(y)} = \frac{w_x \bar{a}_{y_x}^w + w_{x+1} \bar{a}_{y_{x+1}}^w}{2} \tag{6.17}$$

$$C_x^{aw} = D_x^a * q_x^a G_{x(y)} \tag{6.18}$$

$$C_x^{aws} = s_{x+0.5} C_x^{aw} \tag{6.19}$$

Functions based on the active service table, the life table for invalids and the double decrement table for widows/widowers $(b \le x < r)$

$$A_{x(y)} = \frac{\sum_{t=x}^{\omega} D_t^i q_t^i v^{0.5} G_{t(y)}}{D_x^i} \tag{6.20}$$

$$C_x^{iw} = D_x^a * i_x v^{0.5} A_{x+0.5(y)} \tag{6.21}$$

$$C_x^{iws} = s_{x+0.5} C_x^{iw} \tag{6.22}$$

Functions based on the life table for retirees $(r \le x < \omega)$

$$D_x^p = l_x^p u^x \tag{6.23}$$

$$\bar{N}_x^p = \frac{\sum_{t=r}^{\omega} (D_t^p + D_{t+1}^p)}{2} \tag{6.24}$$

$$\bar{a}_x^p = \frac{\bar{N}_x^p}{D_x^p} \tag{6.25}$$

Remark: The above commutation and annuity functions relate to con- tinuously payable salaries and pensions, and may be adequate if payments are made frequently, for example weekly. They can be adjusted to correspond more exactly to any specific payment schedule. For example, if pensions are payable monthly and in arrears, (6.10) should be replaced by (see Appendix 1)

$$a_x^{i(12)} = a_x^i + \frac{11}{24} = \frac{N_{x+1}^i}{D_x^i} + \frac{11}{24}$$

with similar expressions in (6.14) and (6.25).

6.3 EXPRESSIONS FOR PROBABLE PRESENT VALUES OF INSURED SALARIES AND BENEFITS

The following expressions relate to a cohort, of a specific sex, aged x on the date of valuation and refer to a unit insured salary on that date. The expressions for orphans are not indicated but can be derived on the same lines as for widows/ widowers.

Present value of insured salaries $(b \leq x < r)$

$$PVS(x) = \frac{\bar{N}_x^{as} - \bar{N}_r^{as}}{D_x^{as}} \tag{6.26}$$

Present value of retirement pensions

$$PVR(x) = p(r, x) \frac{D_r^{as}}{D_x^{as}} \bar{a}_r^p \tag{6.27}$$

where $p(r, x)$ denotes the retirement pension of the cohort aged x as a propor- tion of the final salary.

Present value of invalidity pensions $(b \leq x < r)$

$$PVI(x) = \frac{\sum_{t=x}^{r-1} p(t, x) C_t^{ais}}{D_x^{as}} \tag{6.28}$$

where $p(t, x)$ denotes the invalidity pension as a proportion of the salary, for an entrant at age x, if invalidity is attained in the age $(t, t+1)$.

Present value of widows'/widowers' pensions (death in service) $(b \leq x < r)$

$$PVW1(x) = RWP \frac{\sum_{t=x}^{r-1} p(t, x) C_t^{aws}}{D_x^{as}} \tag{6.29}$$

Present value of widows'/widowers' pensions (death after invalidity)
$(b \leq x < r)$

$$\text{PVW2}(x) = \text{RWP}\frac{\sum_{t=x}^{r-1} p(t,x)C_t^{iws}}{D_x^{as}} \tag{6.30}$$

Present value of widows'/widowers' pensions (death after retirement)

$$\text{PVW3}(x) = \text{RWP}p(r,x)\frac{D_r^{as}}{D_x^{as}}\frac{\sum_{t=r}^{\omega} D_t^p q_t^p G_{t(y)}}{D_r^p} \tag{6.31}$$

6.4 FURTHER DEVELOPMENT OF THE EXPRESSIONS FOR A SIMPLE PENSION FORMULA

The above expressions, particularly (6.28) to (6.30), can be developed further for any specific pension formula. This is illustrated below for a simple formula where the pension accrues at 1 per cent of the final salary per year. If $ps(x)$ denotes the past service on valuation date,

$$p(r,x) = \frac{ps(x) + r - x}{100} \quad \text{and} \quad p(t,x) = \frac{ps(x) + t - x + 0.5}{100}$$

$$\text{PVI}(x) = \frac{R_{x+1}^{ais} + (ps(x) + 0.5)M_x^{ais}}{100D_x^{as}} \tag{6.32}$$

where

$$M_x^{ais} = \sum_{t=x}^{r-1} C_t^{ais} \tag{6.33}$$

$$R_x^{ais} = \sum_{t=x}^{r-1} M_t^{ais} \tag{6.34}$$

$$\text{PVW1}(x) = \text{RWP}\frac{R_{x+1}^{aws} + (ps(x) + 0.5)M_x^{aws}}{100D_x^{as}} \tag{6.35}$$

where

$$M_x^{aws} = \sum_{t=x}^{r-1} C_t^{aws} \tag{6.36}$$

$$R_x^{aws} = \sum_{t=x}^{r-1} M_t^{aws} \tag{6.37}$$

$$\text{PVW2}(x) = \text{RWP}\frac{R_{x+1}^{iws} + (ps(x) + 0.5)M_x^{iws}}{100D_x^{as}} \tag{6.38}$$

where

$$M_x^{iws} = \sum_{t=x}^{r-1} C_t^{iws} \tag{6.39}$$

$$R_x^{iws} = \sum_{t=x}^{r-1} M_t^{iws} \tag{6.40}$$

6.5 CALCULATION OF AVERAGE PREMIUMS

The application of the present value method is illustrated in this section for computing the average premiums AP1 and AP2, respectively for the initial population and new entrants, and the general average premium, GAP, for a new pension scheme. For simplicity, only one sex is considered; it should be understood that in practice, the results for males and females would need to be pooled.

Let $Ac(x, 0)$ denote the initial population aged x on the valuation date and $s(x, 0)$ the average insured salary of this population. Let $pr(x)$ denote the proportion of new entrants entering at age x – assumed to be the same for all new entrant generations; let $na(t)$ denote the number of new entrants in the tth year $(t - 1, t)$, assumed to enter at the middle of the year; and let $sn(x)$ denote the average insured salary of a standard generation of new entrants entering on the valuation date. Let the probable present values – corresponding to unit initial salary – of salaries and total pensions (all categories combined) relating to the initial population be denoted by PVS1(x) and PVB1(x), and the corresponding quantities for the standard new entrant generation be denoted by PVS2(x) and PVB2(x). The average premiums for the initial population and for new entrants will then be given by

$$\text{AP1} = \frac{\sum_{x=b}^{r-1} Ac(x, 0)s(x, 0)\text{PVB1}(x)}{\sum_{x=b}^{r-1} Ac(x, 0)s(x, 0)\text{PVS1}(x)} \tag{6.41}$$

$$\text{AP2} = \frac{\sum_{x=b}^{r-1} pr(x)sn(x)\text{PVB2}(x)}{\sum_{x=b}^{r-1} pr(x)sn(x)\text{PVS2}(x)} \tag{6.42}$$

If the above expressions are abbreviated as

$$\text{AP1} = P1/Q1 \quad \text{and} \quad \text{AP2} = P2/Q2$$

the general average premium will be given by

$$\text{GAP} = \frac{P1 + kP2}{Q1 + kQ2} \tag{6.43}$$

where k is given by

$$k = \sum_{t=1}^{\infty} na(t)v^{t-0.5} \tag{6.44}$$

and $v = 1/(1+i)$ – see section 6.1, above. The expression for k can be simplified if $na(t)$ is assumed to follow a simple law. For example, if $na(t) = na(1)(1+f)^{t-1}$ then the expression will converge, provided $1+f < 1+i$, to

$$k = na(1)\frac{(1+i)^{0.5}}{(i-f)} \tag{6.45}$$

The above condition for convergence is none other than the well-known condition that the rate of interest must exceed the sum of the rate of growth of the number of new entrants and the rate of escalation of salaries.

APPENDICES

BASIC ACTUARIAL MATHEMATICS

This appendix provides a brief summary of the principal elements of basic actuarial mathematics. It is mainly intended as a source of ready reference. For details, one of the standard basic actuarial textbooks should be consulted (e.g. Hooker and Longley-Cook, 1953 and 1957; Jordan, 1967; Neill, 1986).

1 Compound interest

Interest may be regarded as the reward paid by a *borrower* for the use of an asset, referred to as the *capital* or *principal*, belonging to the *lender*. It is assumed that both capital and interest are measured in units of a given currency.

Interest may be simple or compound. If a capital of C units is lent at *simple interest* at the rate of i per annum for n years, the accumulated sum at the end of the period will be given by

$$AS = C(1 + ni) \tag{A1.1}$$

If, on the other hand, the sum is placed at *compound interest*, the accumulated sum is given by

$$AS = C(1 + i)^n \tag{A1.2}$$

It is the concept of compound interest which underlies the assessment and evaluation of investments. Accordingly, in this appendix the references are uniquely to compound interest.

The above definition of compound interest is based on an annual period. Theoretically, it is possible to conceive of an equivalent *force of interest* δ, assumed to operate continuously. The relationship between δ and i can be expressed as follows:

$$\delta = \log_e(1 + i); \qquad e^\delta = 1 + i \tag{A1.3}$$

The symbol v is often used to denote the reciprocal of $1 + i$. Thus,

$$v = \frac{1}{1 + i} = e^{-\delta} \tag{A1.4}$$

An important concept is that of the *present value* of an accumulated sum due n years hence. This refers to the capital which, if lent (or invested) at the rate of i per annum, will amount to, say K, at the end of the n-year period. It is given by

$$PV = K(1+i)^{-n} = Kv^n = Ke^{-n\delta} \tag{A1.5}$$

When the receipt of the accumulated sum K is subject to a probability p, its present value is called the *probable present value* and is given by

$$PPV = pK e^{-n\delta} \tag{A1.6}$$

The word "probable" is sometimes omitted if it is evident from the context.

2   Financial annuities

Assume that a unit amount is paid at the beginning of each year for n years. This series of payments is referred to as an *annuity-due*.

The present value of the annuity-due is the sum of the present values of the individual payments. It has the following symbol and expression:

$$\ddot{a}_{\overline{n}|} = 1 + v + v^2 + \cdots + v^{n-1} = \frac{1-v^n}{1-v} \tag{A1.7}$$

If the annual payments are made at the *end* of each year, the annuity is called an immediate annuity. It has the following symbol and is related to the annuity-due as indicated:

$$a_{\overline{n}|} = v\ddot{a}_{\overline{n}|} \tag{A1.8}$$

The accumulated value of an annuity is the sum of the accumulated values of the individual payments. For example, the accumulated value of an immediate annuity has the following symbol and expression:

$$s_{\overline{n}|} = (1+i)^{n-1} + (1+i)^{n-2} + \cdots + (1+i) + 1 = (1+i)^n a_{\overline{n}|} \tag{A1.9}$$

More generally, an annuity may be payable in m instalments spread evenly over the year. Depending upon whether the payment is made at the end or the beginning of each fractional period, this annuity is symbolized and evaluated as follows:

$$a_{\overline{n}|}^{(m)} = \frac{i}{i^{(m)}} a_{\overline{n}|} \tag{A1.10}$$

$$\ddot{a}_{\overline{n}|}^{(m)} = a_{\overline{n}|}^{(m)} + \frac{i}{m} a_{\overline{n}|} \tag{A1.11}$$

where

$$i^{(m)} = m[(1+i)^{1/m} - 1] \tag{A1.12}$$

For theoretical purposes, it is possible to conceive of a *continuous annuity*, where a unit amount per year is assumed to be invested continuously over the year. The corresponding present and accumulated values have the following symbols and expressions:

$$\bar{a}_{\overline{n}|} = \frac{1-e^{-\delta n}}{\delta}; \qquad \bar{s}_{\overline{n}|} = \frac{e^{\delta n}-1}{\delta} \tag{A1.13}$$

3   The life table

The life table, also known as the mortality table, is a device for exhibiting mortality data over the human lifespan. It is represented by the function $\{l_x\}$ indicating the survivors to exact integral age x out of a hypothetical initial number of, say, 100,000 newborns. The table is said to be subject to a single *decrement*, that is, death. The range of x is $(0, \omega)$, ω representing the limit of life. An auxiliary function is d_x, which indicates the number of lives eliminated by death between ages x and $x + 1$. It is given by the relationship

$$d_x = l_x - l_{x+1} \tag{A1.14}$$

The *central mortality rate* at age $x(m_x)$ and the *life table mortality rate* (q_x), the latter representing the probability for a person aged x to die within one year, are given by

$$m_x = \frac{2d_x}{l_x + l_{x+1}}; \qquad q_x = \frac{d_x}{l_x} = \frac{2m_x}{2 + m_x} \tag{A1.15}$$

The complement of the life table mortality rate, representing the probability for a person aged x to survive to age $x + 1$, is indicated by the symbol p_x and is given by the relationship

$$p_x = \frac{l_{x+1}}{l_x} = 1 - q_x \tag{A1.16}$$

For theoretical purposes, it is customary to assume that l_x is a continuous function of x. The *force* of mortality at any age x (not necessarily integral), indicated by μ_x, is given by

$$\mu_x = -\frac{1}{l_x}\frac{dl_x}{dx} \tag{A1.17}$$

The force of mortality at age $x + 0.5$ is approximately given by

$$\mu_{x+0.5} = \frac{q_x}{1 - 0.5q_x} \tag{A1.18}$$

The *expectation of life* at age x measures the average future lifetime at that age. The *curtate* expectation, denoted by e_x, represents the average number of full years lived beyond age x while the *complete* expectation, denoted by e_x^o, represents the average exact future lifetime. They are given by the following formulae:

$$e_x = \frac{(l_{x+1} + l_{x+2} + \cdots)}{l_x} \tag{A1.19}$$

$$e_x^o = \frac{1}{l_x}\int_x^\omega l_y \, dy \tag{A1.20}$$

The complete expectation is approximately given by

$$e_x^o = e_x + 0.5 \tag{A1.21}$$

4   Elementary commutation functions

Commutation functions are derived by combining life table functions with compound interest functions. They are used for computing life annuity and assurance functions, discussed in section 5, below.

Commutation functions of level 1, D_x and C_x, are defined as follows ($0 \le x < \omega$):

$$D_x = l_x v^x; \qquad C_x = d_x v^{x+1} \tag{A1.22}$$

Commutation functions of the second level, N_x and M_x, are obtained by summing the corresponding first-level functions, as follows:

$$N_x = \sum_{y=x}^{\omega} D_y; \qquad M_x = \sum_{y=x}^{\omega} C_y \tag{A1.23}$$

Commutation functions of level 3, denoted by S_x and R_x, are obtained by performing similar summations of the second-level functions, and so on.

There are also other commutation functions, used for the theory or the techniques of valuation of pension benefits. These are introduced and defined in Chapters 2, 3 and 6.

5 Life annuities and assurances

A series of payments of one unit at the beginning of each year, payable so long as a life aged x is alive, is called a *life annuity-due*. The probable present value of this annuity has the following symbol, and it can be expressed in terms of the elementary commutation functions as indicated:

$$\ddot{a}_x = \frac{N_x}{D_x} \tag{A1.24}$$

If the payments are made at the end of each year, the annuity is termed an *immediate life annuity*. It is denoted by the symbol a_x and has the following expression:

$$a_x = \frac{N_{x+1}}{D_x} \tag{A1.25}$$

A life annuity, due or immediate, may be payable in m equal instalments spread evenly over the year. It has then the following symbols and the approximate expressions,

$$\ddot{a}_x^{(m)} = \ddot{a}_x - \frac{m-1}{2m} \tag{A1.26}$$

$$a_x^{(m)} = a_x + \frac{m-1}{2m} \tag{A1.27}$$

A continuous life annuity is one where a unit per year is paid continuously over the year. Its probable present value is denoted as follows and has the approximate expression

$$\bar{a}_x = \frac{\bar{N}_x}{D_x} \tag{A1.28}$$

where

$$\bar{N}_x = \frac{N_x + N_{x+1}}{2}$$

If the term of a life annuity is limited to n years, it is termed a *temporary life annuity*. For example, a temporary life annuity-due is denoted by the following symbol and has the expression

$$\ddot{a}_{x:\bar{n}|} = \frac{N_x - N_{x+n}}{D_x} \tag{A1.29}$$

Similarly,

$$a_{x:\bar{n}|} = \frac{N_{x+1} - N_{x+n+1}}{D_x} \tag{A1.30}$$

$$\bar{a}_{x:\bar{n}|} = \frac{\bar{N}_x - \bar{N}_{x+n}}{D_x} \tag{A1.31}$$

Further,

$$a^{(m)}_{x:\bar{n}|} = a_{x:\bar{n}|} + \frac{m-1}{2m}\left[1 - \frac{D_{x+n}}{D_x}\right] \tag{A1.32}$$

$$\ddot{a}^{(m)}_{x:\bar{n}|} = \ddot{a}_{x:\bar{n}|} - \frac{m-1}{2m}\left[1 - \frac{D_{x+n}}{D_x}\right] \tag{A1.33}$$

A *joint life annuity* is one which is payable as long as two lives aged x and y are both alive. If it is payable at the end of each year, it has the following symbol and expression:

$$a_{xy} = \sum_t \frac{l_{x+t}}{l_x}\frac{l_{y+t}}{l_y} v^t \tag{A1.34}$$

where t runs from 1 to the end of the period of payment. An annuity payable to a life aged y after the death of a life aged x is called a *last survivor annuity* and has the symbol and expression

$$a_{x/y} = a_y - a_{xy} \tag{A1.35}$$

If a unit amount is payable at the end of the year in which a life aged x dies, the arrangement is called a *whole life insurance*. The probable present value of the insurance is denoted by A_x and is given by

$$A_x = \frac{M_x}{D_x} \tag{A1.36}$$

An *endowment insurance* is given by the expression

$$A_{x:\bar{n}|} = \frac{M_x - M_{x+n}}{D_x} + \frac{D_{x+n}}{D_x} \tag{A1.37}$$

In this case, the assured amount is paid at the end of the year of death, if death occurs within a term of n years, or on survival to the end of the term. An endowment insurance is seen to be the sum of a *temporary* (or *term*) *insurance* and a *pure endowment*. If the sum assured is payable immediately on death, M_x in the above expressions should be replaced by

$$\bar{M}_x = \frac{M_x + M_{x+1}}{2} \tag{A1.38}$$

and similarly for M_{x+n}.

6 The multiple decrement table

A *multiple decrement table* is similar to a life table except that there is more than one decrement to be considered.

A distinction should be made between the *independent* and *dependent* rates of decrement. The independent rate applies when a decrement is acting alone, while the dependent rate refers to the case where the given decrement is acting concurrently with one or more other decrements. The case of a *double decrement* table subject to two decrements α and β is discussed below and then generalized to three decrements.

Let l_x represent the number of survivors to age x in the double decrement table, $^*\alpha_x$ and $^*\beta_x$ the dependent rates corresponding to the decrements, and α_x and β_x the corresponding independent rates. Then the dependent rates can be expressed in terms of the independent rates, as follows:

$$^*\alpha_x = \alpha_x(1 - \beta_x/2); \qquad ^*\beta_x = \beta_x(1 - \alpha_x/2) \tag{A1.39}$$

If the independent rates are given, the dependent rates can be calculated using the above formulae. The double decrement table functions l_x and the auxiliary functions d_x^α and d_x^β, indicating respectively the number of exits due to causes α and β between ages x and $x + 1$, can be established starting from a hypothetical number, say 100,000 at the youngest age b, using the following formulae successively:

$$d_x^\alpha = l_x {}^*\alpha_x; \qquad d_x^\beta = l_x {}^*\beta_x; \qquad l_{x+1} = l_x - d_x^\alpha - d_x^\beta \tag{A1.40}$$

It will also be apparent that

$$l_{x+1} = l_x(1 - {}^*\alpha_x - {}^*\beta_x) = l_x(1 - \alpha_x)(1 - \beta_x) \tag{A1.41}$$

The above formulae, expressing dependent rates in terms of the independent rates, can be generalized for three decrements α, β and γ, as follows:

$$^*\alpha_x = \alpha_x\left(1 - \frac{(\beta_x + \gamma_x)}{2} + \frac{\beta_x\gamma_x}{3}\right) \tag{A1.42}$$

with similar expressions for $^*\beta_x$ and $^*\gamma_x$

Further,

$$l_{x+1} = l_x(1 - {}^*\alpha_x - {}^*\beta_x - {}^*\gamma_x) = l_x(1 - \alpha_x)(1 - \beta_x)(1 - \gamma_x) \tag{A1.43}$$

The extension of the multiple decrement theory to further decrements can be made on the same lines.

The active service table is an example of a multiple decrement table. It indicates the progress according to age of a cohort of persons covered by a pension scheme, over the age range extending from the age of entry (b) to the age of retirement (r). The active service table for a social security pension scheme normally allows for two decrements: (a) death, and (b) invalidity. Even if retirement can take place over a range of ages, it will still be possible to work with a double decrement table if retirements can be assumed to take place at integral ages; otherwise it will be necessary to adopt a triple decrement table.

The active service table is represented by the function $\{l_x^a\}$, $b \leq x \leq r$, where l_x^a signifies the number of persons continuing to be in active insured status at age x out of an initial hypothetical number of, say, 100,000 entering the scheme at age b. It can be constructed for any given pension scheme after adopting appropriate assumptions for the rates of mortality (q_x) and invalidity (i_x) and, if necessary, of retirement (r_x). The formulae to be used for its construction would depend upon whether the assumptions relate to independent or dependent rates.

NUMERICAL ILLUSTRATIONS

1   A hypothetical pension scheme

In order to illustrate the various financial systems discussed in Chapters 1 and 2, a simple, hypothetical pension scheme has been adopted. Only retirement pensions are considered, payable for life from age 65. The pension formula is 1 per cent of the final salary per year of contributory service. Persons over 65 at the outset are not entitled to any pension.

The Lexis diagram (figure 1) enables the components of the pension scheme and its evolution over time to be visualized.

2   The initial insured population

The initial insured population numbers 10,000 persons, distributed by age as shown in the second column of table 1. This population is used for the demonstration of the projections and the financial systems, in tables 3, 4 and 5. (The distribution in the third column is used for table 7 only – see section 7, below.) The distribution in the second column is a stable age distribution resulting from the demographic assumptions – see section 3, below. Table 1 also shows the average annual starting salaries of the initial population and the pre-scheme service of this population.

3   Demographic assumptions

The intrinsic force of growth of the insured population (ρ) is assumed to be 1 per cent. New entrants are assumed to enter at a single age, 20. The rates of decrement of the insured population are assumed to remain constant, and mortality is the only decrement which is considered. Table 2 shows the service table for active insured persons and the life table for pensioners, corresponding to the assumed rates of decrement.

In order to simplify the computations, the same force of demographic growth, rates of decrement and entry age are assumed to have operated also in the past and for a sufficiently long time, with the consequence that the age distribution of the insured population has become stable when the scheme commences – see section 2, above.

4 Economic assumptions

The relative progression with advancing age of the insured salary for an individual member (the salary scale) is also shown in table 2. In addition, the force of growth of the general level of salaries (γ) is assumed to be 3 per cent. The force of pension indexation (β) is also assumed at 3 per cent. The force of interest (δ) is assumed at 6 per cent.

5 Demographic and financial projections

The demographic and financial projections are made for two variants:

- variant 1: pre-scheme service is not recognized;
- variant 2: pre-scheme service is fully recognized.

The density factor has been assumed at 100 per cent. Administrative expenses have been ignored. The results are shown in table 3. For both variants demographic maturity is reached in 35 years. Financial maturity is reached in 35 years for variant 2 and in 80 years for variant 1. The financial projections are illustrated in figure 2.

6 Demonstration of financial systems

The results of the calculations for variant 1 are given in table 4 and those for variant 2 in table 5. The tables show the time-related contribution rates and reserves at ten-year intervals. Reserves are shown both in monetary units and as a multiple of the corresponding salary bills.

The scaled premium system is demonstrated for variant 1 only. Funding methods for occupational pension schemes are considered for variant 2 only; the initial accrued liability is assumed to be amortized by equal annual instalments over the active lifetime of the youngest initial entrant.

The above results are illustrated in figures 3 to 8 and in figures 11 to 14.

Table 6 presents the age-related contribution rate and reserve functions for the individual actuarial cost methods discussed in Chapter 2. These results are illustrated in figures 9 and 10.

7 Sensitivity of premiums to parametric variations

The sensitivity of selected premiums to changes in the assumptions concerning the determining parameters is illustrated in table 7. These results correspond to variant 2 (full recognition of pre-scheme service).

In order to demonstrate the effect of the variation of the force of demographic growth, for the purpose of this table, the age distribution of the initial population has been assumed independently of any of the simulated forces of demographic growth. This distribution, shown in the third column of table 1, differs slightly from the stable age distribution assumed for the main demonstrations. Therefore, while the results in table 7 are mutually consistent, they are not strictly comparable with those in tables 3, 4 and 5.

Note: The $ sign has been used in tables 1 to 6 to indicate the monetary unit.

Actuarial mathematics of social security pensions

Table 1   The data

Age group	Initial population		Annual salary ($)	Past service (years)
	Tables 3, 4, 5	Table 7		
20–25	1 415	1 478	1 330	2.5
25–30	1 339	1 381	1 940	7.5
30–35	1 265	1 289	2 440	12.5
35–40	1 193	1 201	2 850	17.5
40–45	1 121	1 114	3 160	22.5
45–50	1 047	1 027	3 370	27.5
50–55	967	937	3 480	32.5
55–60	878	840	3 500	37.5
60–65	775	733	3 500	42.5
Total	10 000	10 000		

Table 2   The basis

Active lives			Pensioners	
Age	Service table	Salary scale	Age	Life table
20	1 000	100	65	1 000
25	995	165	70	861
30	989	221	75	677
35	982	267	80	463
40	972	302	85	254
45	958	328	90	101
50	936	344	95	25
55	903	350	100	0
60	851	350		
65	775	350		

Table 3 Projections

Year	Numbers			Amounts				
	Actives	Pensioners	Ratio (%)	Salary bill ($ '000)	Variant 1 Expenditure ($ '000)	Variant 1 PAYG (%)	Variant 2 Expenditure ($ '000)	Variant 2 PAYG (%)
1	10 000	0	0	27 188	0	0	0	0
11	11 052	1 294	11.71	40 522	328	0.81	2 748	6.78
21	12 214	2 137	17.50	60 451	1 665	2.75	6 127	10.14
31	13 499	2 537	18.79	90 184	4 616	5.12	9 819	10.89
41	14 918	2 811	18.84	134 538	10 150	7.54	14 685	10.92
51	16 487	3 107	18.84	200 709	19 574	9.75	21 907	10.92
61	18 221	3 433	18.84	299 422	32 054	10.71	32 685	10.92
71	20 138	3 795	18.84	446 687	48 706	10.90	48 758	10.92
81	22 255	4 194	18.84	666 380	72 742	10.92	72 742	10.92

Note: Numbers and amounts "in force" at the beginning of the year indicated.

Table 4a Variant 1: GAP, TFS and AFS systems

Year	GAP			TFS			AFS		
	Contribution rate (%)	Reserves ($ million)	Multiple of salary bill	Contribution rate (%)	Reserves ($ million)	Multiple of salary bill	Contribution rate (%)	Reserves ($ million)	Multiple of salary bill
1	6.08	0	0	0	0	0	6.53	0	0
11	6.08	26	0.64	2.05	3	0.08	6.41	28	0.69
21	6.08	77	1.27	4.10	15	0.25	6.24	82	1.35
31	6.08	162	1.79	6.14	39	0.43	6.06	172	1.90
41	6.08	292	2.17	8.19	84	0.62	5.89	308	2.29
51	6.08	473	2.36	9.22	159	0.79	5.83	499	2.48
61	6.08	723	2.41	9.22	253	0.85	5.83	760	2.54
71	6.08	1 081	2.42	9.22	379	0.85	5.83	1 136	2.54
81	6.08	1 613	2.42	9.22	566	0.85	5.83	1 695	2.54

Notes: AP1 = 6.53 per cent; AP2 = 5.83 per cent. TFS and AFS contribution rates at the beginning of the year indicated. Reserves at the beginning of the year indicated.

Table 4b Variant 1: SCP1 and SCP2 systems

	SCP1					SCP2			
Period (years)	Contribution rate (%)	Year	Reserves ($ million)	Multiple of salary bill	Period (years)	Contribution rate (%)	Year	Reserves ($ million)	Multiple of salary bill
		1	0	0			1	0	0
01:20	1.65	11	6	0.15	01:20	2.15	11	8	0.21
		21	11	0.18			21	18	0.31
21:40	5.35	31	35	0.39	21:40	6.09	31	56	0.62
		41	49	0.37			41	98	0.73
41:60	8.61	51	89	0.44	41:60	8.82	51	182	0.91
		61	105	0.35			61	282	0.94
61:80	9.63	71	131	0.29	61:80	9.02	71	425	0.95
		81	145	0.22			81	634	0.95
81 +	10.49				81 +	9.02			

Notes: SCP contribution rates for the 20-year period indicated. Reserves at the beginning of the year indicated.

Table 5a Variant 2: GAP/TFS and AFS systems

	GAP/TFS			AFS		
Year	Contribution rate (%)	Reserves ($ million)	Multiple of salary bill	Contribution rate (%)	Reserves ($ million)	Multiple of salary bill
1	9.22	0	0	15.32	0	0
11	9.22	25	0.63	13.76	50	1.23
21	9.22	50	0.82	11.49	118	1.94
31	9.22	77	0.85	9.02	211	2.34
41	9.22	114	0.85	6.78	339	2.52
51	9.22	170	0.85	5.83	511	2.54
61	9.22	254	0.85	5.83	762	2.54
71	9.22	379	0.85	5.83	1 136	2.54
81	9.22	566	0.85	5.83	1 695	2.54

Note: AP1 = 15.32 per cent; AP2 = 5.83 per cent. AFS contribution rates and reserves at the beginning of the year indicated.

Table 5b Variant 2: ACC1 and ACC2 systems

Year	ACC1			ACC2		
	Contribution rate (%)	Reserves ($ million)	Multiple of salary bill	Contribution rate (%)	Reserves ($ million)	Multiple of salary bill
1	13.99	0	0	16.18	0	0
11	11.71	42	1.02	12.85	49	1.21
21	10.18	91	1.50	10.61	109	1.81
31	9.15	155	1.72	9.12	191	2.12
41	8.47	251	1.87	8.12	314	2.33
51	7.07	387	1.93	6.08	486	2.42
61	7.07	578	1.93	6.08	724	2.42
71	7.07	863	1.93	6.08	1 081	2.42
81	7.07	1 288	1.93	6.08	1 612	2.42

Note: Initial accrued liability in $ million: ACC1, 29; ACC2, 43. Contribution rates and reserves at the beginning of the year indicated. Contributions include "normal" contributions and payments towards the amortization of the initial accrued liability.

Table 5c Variant 2: ENT and AGG systems

Year	ENT			AGG		
	Contribution rate (%)	Reserves ($ million)	Multiple of salary bill	Contribution rate (%)	Reserves ($ million)	Multiple of salary bill
1	16.73	0	0	15.32	0	0
11	13.13	51	1.25	12.45	46	1.14
21	10.73	114	1.88	10.45	102	1.69
31	9.11	200	2.22	9.05	178	1.97
41	8.03	330	2.45	8.07	288	2.14
51	5.83	511	2.54	7.39	454	2.26
61	5.83	762	2.54	6.92	703	2.35
71	5.83	1 136	2.54	6.59	1 076	2.41
81	5.83	1 695	2.54	6.36	1 632	2.45

Notes: Initial accrued liability in $ million: ENT, 46. Contribution rates and reserves at the beginning of the year indicated. Contributions include "normal" contributions and payments towards the amortization of the initial accrued liability.

Table 6 Age-related contribution rate and reserve functions (cohort entering at $t = 0$)

Age	ACC1			ACC2			ENT		
	Contribution rate (%)	Reserves ($ '000)	% of terminal reserves	Contribution rate (%)	Reserves ($ '000)	% of terminal reserves	Contribution rate (%)	Reserves ($ '000)	% of terminal reserves
20	0.57	0	0	7.78	0	0	5.83	0	0
25	1.18	7	0.13	5.51	52	1.00	5.83	48	0.92
30	1.86	31	0.59	4.80	141	2.70	5.83	146	2.80
35	2.78	89	1.71	4.65	287	5.51	5.83	316	6.06
40	3.93	210	4.03	4.83	517	9.92	5.83	586	11.24
45	5.54	448	8.59	5.24	872	16.73	5.83	994	19.07
50	7.73	885	16.98	5.94	1 413	27.11	5.83	1 589	30.48
55	10.94	1 648	31.61	7.04	2 225	42.68	5.83	2 433	46.67
60	16.43	2 955	56.69	8.67	3 433	65.85	5.83	3 605	69.15
65	26.02	5 213		11.07	5 213		5.83	5 213	

Table 7 Sensitivity of premiums to parametric changes

Simulation	Parameters (%)				Premiums (%)			
(a) General case								
	ρ	δ	γ	β	GAP	PAYG*	AP2*	TFS*
1	1.00	6.00	3.00	2.75	8.82	10.68	5.71	9.03
2	1.00	6.25	3.00	2.75	8.63	10.68	5.27	8.85
3	1.00	5.75	3.00	2.75	9.02	10.68	6.19	9.21
4	1.10	6.00	3.00	2.75	8.72	10.36	5.71	8.84
5	0.90	6.00	3.00	2.75	8.93	11.01	5.71	9.22
6	1.00	6.00	3.25	2.75	8.84	10.45	6.07	9.03
7	1.00	6.00	2.75	2.75	8.81	10.92	5.37	9.03
8	1.00	6.00	3.00	3.00	9.00	10.92	5.83	9.21
9	1.00	6.00	3.00	2.50	8.65	10.45	5.60	8.85
(b) Under wage indexation								
	ρ	$\delta-\gamma$			GAP	PAYG*	AP2*	TFS*
10	1.00	3.00			9.00	10.92	5.83	9.21
11	1.00	3.25			8.81	10.92	5.37	9.03
12	1.00	2.75			9.21	10.92	6.32	9.40
13	1.10	3.00			8.90	10.59	5.83	9.02
14	0.90	3.00			9.10	11.25	5.83	9.41

Note: ρ = force of population growth; δ = force of interest; γ = force of salary escalation; β = force of pension indexation.

Figure 1 The Lexis diagram

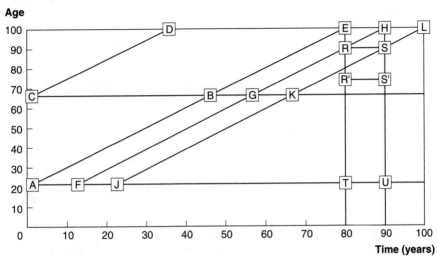

Figure 2 Benefit expenditure as a percentage of insured salary bill

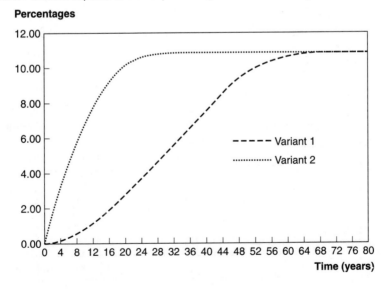

Figure 3. Variant 1: PAYG, GAP, TFS and AFS systems – contribution rates

Percentages

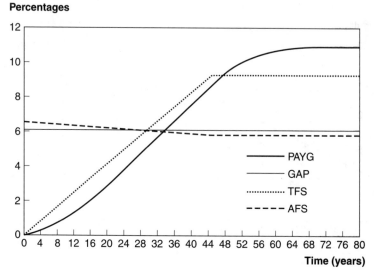

Figure 4. Variant 2: PAYG, GAP, TFS and AFS systems – contribution rates

Percentages

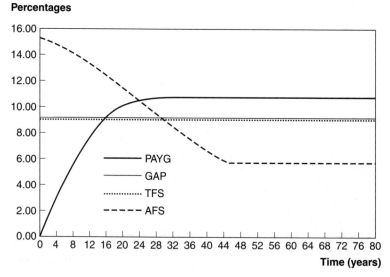

Figure 5. Variant 1: GAP, TFS and AFS systems – reserves as a multiple of salary bill

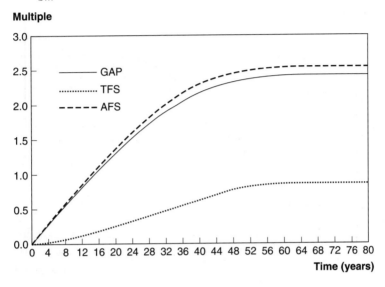

Figure 6. Variant 2: GAP, TFS and AFS systems – reserves as a multiple of salary bill

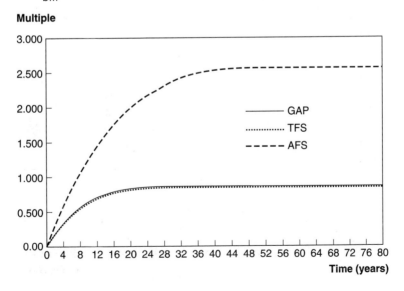

Figure 7. Variant 1: The scaled premium system (compared with PAYG and GAP) – contribution rates

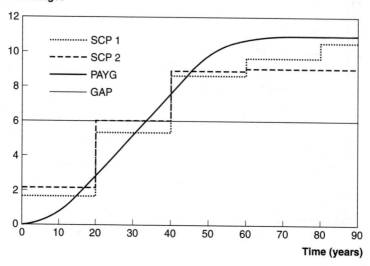

Figure 8. Variant 2: The scaled premium system (compared with GAP) – reserves as a multiple of salary bill

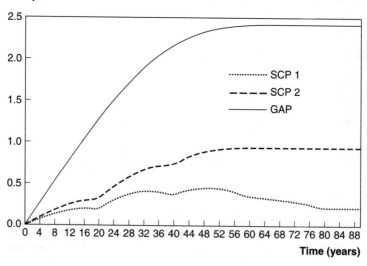

Figure 9. Individual cost methods: Age-related contribution rate function

Percentages

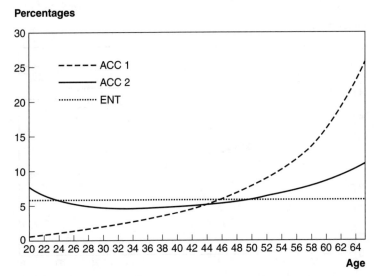

Figure 10. Individual cost methods: Age-related reserve function (expressed as a percentage of terminal reserve)

Percentages

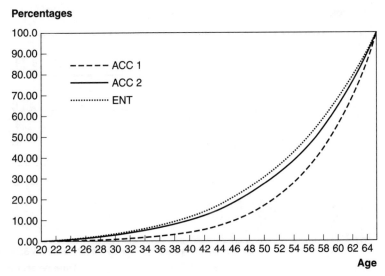

Figure 11. Variant 2: Individual cost methods (compared with GAP) – contribution rates

Percentages

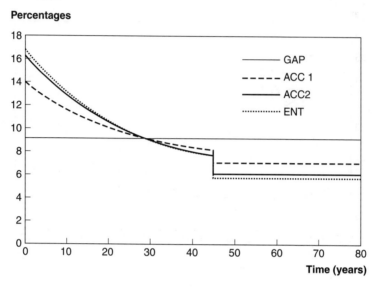

Figure 12. Variant 2: Individual cost methods (compared with GAP) – reserves as a multiple of salary bill

Multiple

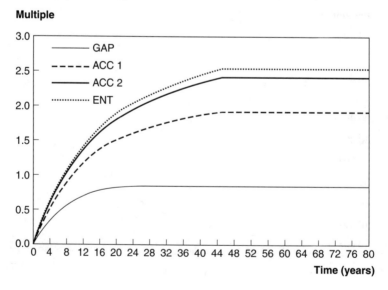

Figure 13.   Variant 2: Aggregate cost method (compared with AFS, ENT and GAP) –
contribution rates

Percentages

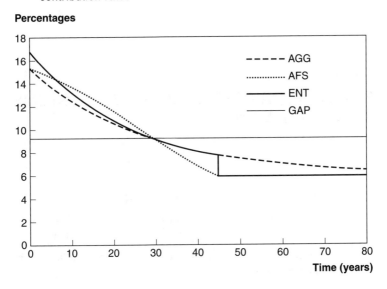

Figure 14.   Variant 2: Aggregate cost method (compared with AFS, ENT and GAP) –
reserves as a multiple of salary bill

Multiple

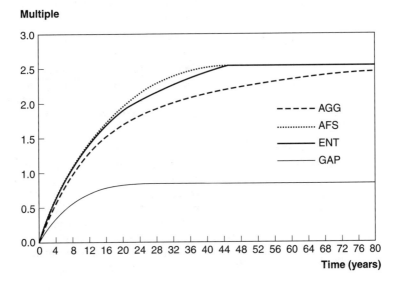

GLOSSARY OF PRINCIPAL FINANCIAL SYSTEMS AND FUNDING METHODS

Acronym	Full title	Brief description
PAYG	Pay as you go	Contributions exactly balance expenditures in selected time intervals (e.g. annually)
GAP	General average premium system	Contribution rate remains level ad infinitum
AFS	"Autonomous funding system"	Initial population and new entrants constitute separate autonomous risk pools, applying respective average premiums (AP1 and AP2) as contribution rate
TFS	Terminal funding system	Contributions exactly balance capital value of new pension awards in selected time intervals (e.g. annually)
SCP	Scaled premium system	Steadily increasing level contribution rates in successive intervals, with a non-decreasing reserve fund. Specific variants: the reserve attains a local maximum (SCP1) or attains the growth rate of the financially mature situation. (SCP2) at the end of each interval
ACC	Accrued benefit method	Age-related contribution rate determined such that for new entrants, age-related reserve fund equals accrued benefits based on current service and current (ACC1) or projected (ACC2) salary, allowing for pension indexation. Initial accrued liability funded separately (e.g. through uniform payments spread over active lifetime of youngest initial entrant)

Acronym	Full title	Brief description
ENT	Entry age method	For new entrants, benefit funded through level contribution rate over active lifetime. Initial accrued liability funded as for ACC
AGG	Aggregate method	Time-related contribution rate is that which produces the closed-fund actuarial balance at that time

LIST OF SYMBOLS

The following is a list of the special symbols which have been adopted for the purposes of this book, in the order in which they are introduced. Basic actuarial symbols and functions are not included here, but will be found in Appendix 1. Similarly, the special commutation functions used in Chapter 6 for the application of the present value technique, which have been largely standardized in actuarial literature, are not reproduced.

Chapter 1

δ	Force of interest
ρ	Force of growth of new entrants
γ	Force of escalation of insured salaries
β	Force of pension indexation
μ_x^d	Force of mortality at age x
μ_x^i	Force of invalidity at age x
θ	Force of inflation
$A(t)$	Active population function
$R(t)$	Retired population function
$S(t)$	Insured salary function
$B(t)$	Expenditure function
ω	Limit of life
ω_1	Time of attainment of demographic maturity by pension scheme
ω_2	Time of attainment of financial maturity by pension scheme
$C(t)$	Contribution rate function, time related
$V(t)$	Reserve function, time related
PAYG	Pay-as-you-go financial system
PAYG_n	PAYG contribution rate for the nth financial year
GAP	General average premium system (GAP contribution rate)
$B1(t)$	Expenditure function for the initial population
$B2(t)$	Expenditure function for new entrants
$S1(t)$	Insured salary function for the initial population
$S2(t)$	Insured salary function for new entrants
AP1	Average premium for the initial population

AP2	Average premium for new entrants
AFS	"Autonomous funding system"
$Ka(t)$	Capitalized value of pensions awarded at time t
TFS	Terminal funding system
TFS(t)	Terminal funding system contribution rate function
κ	"Reserve ratio"
λ	"Balance ratio"
SCP	Scaled premium system (variants, SCP1 and SCP2)
PAYG*	Pay-as-you-go premium in the financially mature situation
$\pi(n,m)$	Scaled premium system contribution rate for the interval (n,m)

Chapter 2

$K(x)$	Age-related contribution rate function of a cohort
$F(x)$	Age-related reserve function of a cohort, per unit salary at entry
b	Entry age of a cohort (more generally, lowest entry age)
r	Retirement age of a cohort (more generally, highest retirement age)
s_x	Relative salary scale function
l_x^a	Survival function for active persons
l_x^p	Survival function for retired persons
$D_x^{as(\alpha)}$	Commutation function of level 1, based on the active survival function and force of interest α, and incorporating the salary scale function
$\bar{N}_x^{as(\alpha)}$	Commutation function of level 2, integral of the level 1 function over the range (x,r)
$\bar{a}_x^{p(\alpha)}$	Continuously payable life annuity, based on the life table for pensioners and on force of interest α
ACC1	Accrued benefit cost method 1
ACC2	Accrued benefit cost method 2
ENT	Entry age cost method
AGG	Aggregate cost method

Chapter 3

$Ac(x,t)$	Active population function, age and time related
$Re(x,t)$	Retired population function, age and time related
$Sa(x,t)$	Insured salary function, age and time related
$Be(x,t)$	Expenditure function, age and time related
$\bar{a}_{x:\bar{n}|}^{as(\alpha)}$	Continuous fixed-term life annuity, based on the service table for active persons and on force of interest α, the amount of the annuity increasing from unity in line with the salary scale
AP2*	Average premium for new entrants ($=$ AP2)
TFS*	Terminal funding premium in the mature situation
GAP*	General average premium under wage indexation
ADTS	Average discounted term of insured salaries
ADTB	Average discounted term of expenditures
$\lambda(x)$	Contribution density function
$\lambda_1, \lambda_2, \lambda_3$	Weighted averages of contribution density
$B_a(z)$	Expenditure at time z ($> t$) on pensions in payment at time t

$B_b(z)$	Expenditure at time z ($> t$) on pensions awarded after time t
$V_b(t)$	Reserve for pensioners at time t
$V_a(t)$	Reserve for active persons at time t
$\delta(u)$	The force of interest regarded as a function of time
ϕ	"Real" force of interest ($= \delta - \gamma$)

Chapter 4

γ^*	Force of growth of salary, incorporating escalation and salary scale effects
ϕ^*	Difference between force of growth of salary and force of interest ($\gamma^* - \delta$)

Chapter 5

$Fd(n)$	Value placed on the reserve at time n
n_t	Vector of demographic projection aggregates
Q_t	Matrix of one-year transition probabilities
$I(t)$	Invalidity pensioners function
$W(t)$	Widow/widower pensioners function
$O(t)$	Orphan pensioners function
$p_x^{(rr)}$	Transition probability, status r to r
$q_x^{(rs)}$	Transition probability, status r to s
l_x^i	Survival function for invalids
r^*	Lowest retirement age
l_x^w	Survival function for widows/widowers
y^*	Youngest age of a widow/widower
l_x^o	Survival function for orphan pensioners
z^*	Age limit for orphans' pensions
w_x	Proportion married at age x
y_x	Average age of the spouse
n_x	Average number of orphans of a person dying at age x
z_x	Average age of the orphans
$Act(x, s, t)$	Active population function, age, service and time related
$In(x, t)$	Invalid pensioner function, age and time related
$Wi(x, t)$	Widow/widower pensioner function, age and time related
$N(x, t)$	New entrant function, age and time (year) related
$Z(x, t)$	Active survivors from $N(x, t)$ at the end of the year of entry
$pr(x)$	Proportionate age distribution of new entrant generation
$\gamma(t)$	Rate of salary escalation in projection year t
$\beta(t)$	Rate of pension indexation in projection year t
$i(t)$	Rate of investment return in projection year t
$dc(x)$	Contribution density at age x
$db(x)$	Benefit density at age x
$j(t)$	Adjustment factor for projecting the relative salary function
$s(x, t)$	Average salary function, age and time related
$sn(x, t)$	Average salary function for new entrants
$\Phi(x)$	Distribution function of the standard normal variate
$s1(x, t)$	Average salary function, low income group

$s2(x,t)$	Average salary function, medium income group
$s3(x,t)$	Average salary function, high income group
$ss(x,t)$	Relative salary function
$b(x,t)$	Average benefit function
$sv(x,t)$	Accumulated service function
$IA(t)$	Active population function, initial population projections
$NA(t)$	Active population function, standard new entrant projections
$IR(t)$	Pensioner population function, initial population projections
$NR(t)$	Pensioner population function, standard new entrant projections
$TR(t)$	Total pensioner population function
$na(t)$	Number of new entrants in t^{th} projection year
$TS(t)$	Total insured salaries, at end of tth projection year.
$TP(t)$	Total pensions, at end of tth projection year.
$ADJ(t)$	Adjustment factor for binding
S_t	Insured salary bill, projection year t
B_t	Total expenditure, projection year t
DS_t	Insured salary bill of year t, discounted to valuation date
DB_t	Total expenditure of year t, discounted to valuation date
TDS_t	Cumulated sum of discounted salary bills
TDB_t	Cumulated sum of discounted total expenditures

Chapter 6

$PVS(x)$	Probable present value of insured salaries
$PVR(x)$	Probable present value of retirement pensions
$PVI(x)$	Probable present value of invalidity pensions
$PVW1(x)$	Probable present value of widows'/widowers' pensions (death in service)
$PVW2(x)$	Probable present value of widows'/widowers' pensions (death after invalidity)
$PVW3(x)$	Probable present value of widows'/widowers' pensions (death after retirement)
$p(r,x)$	Retirement pension rate, for cohort aged x on valuation date
$p(t,x)$	Invalidity pension rate at age t, for cohort aged x on valuation date
$ps(x)$	Past service on valuation date
$sn(x)$	Average insured salary of standard new entrant generation on valuation date

APPENDIX 5

THE VARIANT SCP1 OF THE SCALED PREMIUM SYSTEM

This appendix is concerned with the specific variant of the scaled premium system, under which the level premium in any interval (n, m) is positive and leads to a positive non-decreasing reserve fund, reaching a local maximum at the end of the interval. It is shown that the two conditions

$$B'(t) > 0 \tag{A5.1a}$$

$$\frac{B'(t)}{B(t)} \geq \frac{S'(t)}{S(t)} \tag{A5.1b}$$

are, together, sufficient for the existence of this variant. It will be noted that the second condition can also be expressed as

$$\frac{d}{dt}\left(\frac{B(t)}{S(t)}\right) \geq 0 \tag{A5.2}$$

which implies that the pay-as-you-go premium is a non-decreasing function of t. It should also be noted that in view of (A5.1b), $S'(t) > 0$ implies $B'(t) > 0$, but not vice versa. Therefore, (A5.1a) leaves the sign of $S'(t)$ uncertain, that is, $S(t)$ might be an increasing or a decreasing function.

The required result is proved by induction, in three stages. Assuming that SCP1 exists for the interval preceding a specific interval (n, m), it is shown to exist for that interval. It is then easily shown that the system exists for the first interval $(0, p)$. It therefore follows that SCP1 exists for the whole time-range of the pension scheme.

THEOREM 1

Statement: if the conditions (A5.1a) and (A5.1b) are satisfied in the interval (n,m), the function

$$\pi(t) = \frac{B(t)\,e^{-\delta t} + \delta \int_n^t B(z)\,e^{-\delta z}\,dz - \delta V(n)\,e^{-\delta n}}{S(t)\,e^{-\delta t} + \delta \int_n^t S(z)\,e^{-\delta z}\,dz} \tag{A5.3}$$

where $V(n)$ denotes the reserve at the beginning of the interval, is positive and an increasing function of t in the interval, provided the SCP1 system exists in the preceding interval.

Proof: Let the reserve under the application of $\pi(t)$ in (n, t) be denoted by $R(u, t)$, $n \le u \le t$, given by

$$R(u, t) e^{-\delta u} = V(n) e^{-\delta n} + \pi(t) \int_n^u S(z) e^{-\delta z}\, dz - \int_n^u B(z) e^{-\delta z}\, dz \qquad (A5.4)$$

It will be noted that expression (A5.3) is, in fact, the usual formula for the SCP1 premium for the interval (n, t), which can be derived by putting $u = t$ in the fundamental differential equation for the interval (n, t) – expressed as a partial differential equation in the present context – that is,

$$\frac{\partial R(u, t)}{\partial u} = \partial R(u, t) + \pi(t) S(u) - B(u) \qquad (A5.5)$$

equating it to zero, and substituting for $R(u, t)$ in (A5.4).

Let the numerator and denominator of (A5.3) be denoted by $N(t)$ and $D(t)$. Then $D(t) > 0$; and $N(t) > 0$ provided $\delta V(n) < B(n)$, where $V(n)$, being the starting reserve for the interval (n, m), is equally the ending reserve of the previous interval, say (q, n) (see note 1). Since, by assumption, SCP1 exists in the previous interval, π^*, the level-premium in that interval is positive and satisfies the condition

$$\delta V(n) + \pi^* S(n) - B(n) = 0 \qquad (A5.6)$$

which implies $\delta V(n) < B(n)$ This ensures that $\pi(t) > 0$.

Differentiating (A5.3) w.r.t. t and simplifying,

$$\pi'(t) D(t)^2\, e^{\delta t} = D(t) B'(t) - N(t) S'(t) \qquad (A5.7)$$

It can be shown (see note 2) that the PAYG premium at the end of the interval (n,t) exceeds $\pi(t)$, that is

$$\frac{B(t)}{S(t)} > \frac{N(t)}{D(t)} \qquad (A5.8)$$

Multiplying both sides by $S(t)D(t)$ which, being positive, does not change the sign

$$B(t)D(t) > S(t)N(t)$$

It will be noted that both sides of the above inequality are positive. Therefore,

$$\frac{1}{N(t)S(t)} > \frac{1}{B(t)D(t)}$$

Also, multiplying both sides of (A5.1b) by $S(t)B(t)$, which being positive, does not change the sign

$$B'(t) \ge S(t)S'(t)B(t)$$

Note that the left-hand side of the above inequality is positive, in view of (A5.1a). Hence, multipling both sides by the corresponding sides of the previous inequality – which has positive elements on both sides – will not change the sign. Therefore,

$$\frac{B'(t)}{N(t)} > \frac{S'(t)}{D(t)}$$

Multiplying both sides by $N(t)D(t)$ which, being positive, will not change the sign

$$D(t)B'(t) > N(t)S'(t) \qquad \text{(A5.9)}$$

Hence, from (A5.7), $\pi'(t) > 0$. This proves that $\pi(t)$ is an increasing function of t.

THEOREM 2

Statement: Let $V(t)$ $(= R(t,m)$ in the notation of Theorem 1) denote the reserve resulting from the application of the premium $\pi(m)$ in the interval (n,m). Then $V(t)$ is an increasing function, that is, $V'(t) > 0$ for $n < t < m$, and $V'(m) = 0$.

Proof: The fundamental differential equation at any point within the interval (n,m) can be written as

$$V'(t) = \delta V(t) + \pi(m)S(t) - B(t)$$

where $V(t)$ is given by

$$V(t)\,e^{-\delta t} = V(n)\,e^{-\delta n} + \pi(m)\int_n^t S(z)\,e^{-\delta z}\,dz - \int_n^t B(z)\,e^{-\delta z}\,dz$$

Eliminating $V(t)$ between the above two equations and simplifying,

$$V'(t) = e^{\delta t}D(t)[\pi(m) - \pi(t)] \qquad \text{(A5.10)}$$

In view of Theorem 1, it follows that $V'(t) > 0$ for $n < t < m$ and that $V'(m) = 0$.

Incidentally, it will also be obvious that if $V(n) > 0$, then $V(t) > 0$ for $n < t < m$. But $V(n) = V(0) = 0$ in the first interval $(0,p)$. Therefore, in general, $V(t) > 0$.

THEOREM 3

Statement: If π^* denotes the SCP1 premium in a preceding interval (q,n), $\pi(m) > \pi^*$.

Proof: From note 1, it can be seen that

$$Lt_{t \to n+}(\pi(t)) = \frac{B(n) - \delta V(n)}{S(n)}$$

In view of Theorem 1, $\pi'(t) > 0$. Therefore,

$$\pi(t) > \frac{B(n) - \delta V(n)}{S(n)}$$

Now, in view of (A5.6)

$$\pi^* = \frac{B(n) - \delta V(n)}{S(n)}$$

Hence, $\pi(t) > \pi^*$, and in particular,

$$\pi(m) > \pi^*$$

CONCLUSION

Starting from the conditions (A5.1a) and (A5.1b) and the assumption that SCP1 exists in the interval preceding (n, m), Theorem 1 was established. Theorem 2, which follows from Theorem 1, showed that, if the premium over the interval (n, m) is determined according to the formula (A5.3), the reserve function increases over the interval and reaches a local maximum at the end of the interval. Further, Theorem 3 showed that the premium determined according to this formula is greater than the premium determined according to the same formula in the preceding interval.

In the first interval $(0, p)$, the starting reserve $V(0) = 0$, and Theorems 1 and 2 can be proved on the same lines. Theorem 3 does not apply in the first interval. Since $V(0) = 0$, the SCP1 premium in $(0, p)$ is positive (see A5.3).

It therefore follows by induction that under the conditions (A5.1a) and (A5.1b), SCP1 exists for the whole time-range of the pension scheme.

It is emphasized that the conditions (A5.1a) and (A5.1b) have been proved to be sufficient for SCP1 to exist. They may not be necessary for its existence.

Incidentally, it was also proved that the premium function $\pi(t)$ and the reserve function $V(t)$ are both positive.

Note 1: $N'(t) = B'(t) e^{-\delta t}$. Similarly, $D'(t) = S'(t) e^{-\delta t}$.
Therefore $N'(t) > 0$.

$$Lt._{t \to n+}(N(t)) = (B(n) - \delta V(n)) e^{-\delta n}$$

Therefore $N(t) > 0$ if $\delta V(n) < B(n)$.

Note 2: From (A5.3) it will be seen that $\pi(t)$ can be regarded as the weighted average of $B(t)/S(t)$ and

$$AVP(t) = \frac{\int_n^t B(z) e^{-\delta z} \, dz - V(n) e^{-\delta n}}{\int_n^t S(z) e^{-\delta z} \, dz}$$

In view of (A5.2),

$$\frac{B(t)}{S(t)} \geq \frac{\int_n^t B(z) e^{-\delta z} \, dz}{\int_n^t S(z) e^{-\delta z} \, dz} > AVP(t)$$

It therefore follows that

$$\frac{B(t)}{S(t)} > \pi(t) > AVP(t)$$

APPENDIX 6

APPLICATION OF THE LOGNORMAL DISTRIBUTION

Let y denote the salary and let $z = \log_e y$, where $0 < y < \infty$ and $-\infty < z < \infty$. It is assumed that y has the lognormal distribution, or in other words, z has the normal distribution. Let the parameters of the distribution of z be denoted by μ and σ^2. The probability density function of z is

$$p(z) = \frac{1}{\sigma\sqrt{2\pi}} \exp\left(-\frac{(z-\mu)^2}{2\sigma^2}\right) \tag{A6.1}$$

The parameters of the distribution of y can be expressed in terms of integrals of the distribution of z, simplified and then expressed in terms of the distribution function of the standard normal variate. By this procedure the expressions (5.27) and (5.28) of Chapter 5 for the mean and variance of y can be derived. These are standard results.

The same procedure can be applied to derive expression (5.31) for the average of y in the interval (y_a, y_b). Let z_a and z_b denote the corresponding values of z. Let $F(y)$ and $G(y)$ denote the distribution functions of y and z. Then,

$$F(y_b) - F(y_a) = G(z_b) - G(z_a) \tag{A6.2}$$

The required average, denoted by A, is given by

$$A = \frac{\int_{y_a}^{y_b} y\, p(y)\, dy}{F(y_b) - F(y_a)} \tag{A6.3}$$

Changing the variable to z in the numerator,

$$A = \frac{\int_{z_a}^{z_b} e^z p(z)\, dz}{G(z_b) - G(z_a)} \tag{A6.4}$$

The integrand of the numerator which, in view of (A6.1), has the expression

$$\frac{1}{\sigma\sqrt{2\pi}} \exp\left(-\frac{(z-\mu)^2}{2\sigma^2} + z\right) \tag{A6.5}$$

can be simplified as

$$\frac{1}{\sigma\sqrt{2\pi}} \exp\left(\mu + \frac{\sigma^2}{2}\right) \exp\left(-\frac{(z-\mu-\sigma^2)^2}{2\sigma^2}\right) \tag{A6.6}$$

124

By changing to the standardized variable t,

$$t = \frac{z - \mu}{\sigma} - \sigma$$

and noting – see (5.28) – that the overall mean of the distribution of y, say B, is

$$B = \exp\left(\mu + \frac{\sigma^2}{2}\right)$$

It follows that A can be expressed, in terms of B and the distribution function $\Phi(t)$ of the standard normal variate, as

$$A = B\frac{\Phi(w_b - \sigma) - \Phi(w_a - \sigma)}{\Phi(w_b) - \Phi(w_a)} \tag{A6.7}$$

where

$$w_a = \frac{z_a - \mu}{\sigma}$$

and

$$w_b = \frac{z_b - \mu}{\sigma}.$$

BIBLIOGRAPHY

Aaron, Henry. 1966. "The social insurance paradox", in *Canadian Journal of Economics and Political Science* (Toronto, University of Toronto Press), Vol. XXXII, No. 3.

Beattie, Roger; McGillivray, Warren. 1995. "A risky strategy: Reflections on the World Bank Report, *Averting the old age crisis*", in *International Social Security Review* (Geneva, ISSA), 3–4/95.

Bowers, Newton L.; Gerber, Hans U.; Hickman, James C; Jones, Donald A.; Nesbitt, Cecil J. 1986 and 1997(second edition). *Actuarial mathematics* (Itasca, Illinois, Society of Actuaries).

Boye, S. 1971. "Actuarial calculations relating to widows' pensions based on relative age distributions of widows as compared with average ages of widows", in ISSA: *Proceedings of the Fifth International Conference of Social Security Actuaries and Statisticians* (Berne).

Crescentini Laura; Spandonaro, Frederico. 1992. "Methodological developments in forecasting techniques", in ISSA: *Quantitative analysis and the plannning of social protection* (Geneva).

Daykin, Christopher D. 1996. "Actuarial and financial problems associated with the development of complementary pension schemes", in ISSA, 1996.

——; Pentikainen, T.; Pesonen, M. 1994. *Practical risk theory for actuaries* (London, Chapman and Hall).

Ferrara, Giovanna; Drouin, Anne. 1996. "Observations on actuarial concepts used in a simplified pension model", in ISSA, 1996.

Gillion, Colin; Bonilla, Alejandro. 1992. "Analysis of a national private pension scheme: The case of Chile", in *International Labour Review* (Geneva, ILO), Vol. 131, No. 2.

Hirose, Kenichi. 1996. "A generalisation of the concept of the scaled premium", in ISSA, 1996.

Hooker, P.F.; Longley-Cook, L.H. 1953(Vol. 1) and 1957(Vol. 2). *Life and other contingencies* (Cambridge, Institute of Actuaries and Faculty of Actuaries).

International Labour Office (ILO). 1984. *Introduction to social security* (Geneva, 3rd ed.).

——. 1996. *ILO-DIST: The ILO wage distribution model* (Geneva); mimeographed.

——. 1997. *ILO-PENS: The ILO pension model* (Geneva); mimeographed.

International Social Security Association (ISSA). 1996. *Social security financing: Issues and perspectives* (Geneva).

Iyer, S.N. 1971. "The role of national provident funds and pension schemes in capital formation", in ISSA: *Proceedings of the Fifth International Conference of Social Security Actuaries and Statisticians* (Berne).

——. 1993. "Pension reform in developing countries", in *International Labour Review*, Vol. 132, No. 2.

——; McGillivray, W. 1988. "The influence of variations in the level of employment and recent retirement policies on the financing of pension schemes", in ISSA: *Current problems of pensions schemes* (Geneva).

Jordan, Chester Wallace, Jr. 1967. *Society of Actuaries' textbook on life contingencies* (Chicago, Illinois, Society of Actuaries; 2nd ed.).

Lee, E.M. 1986. *An introduction to pension schemes* (London, Institute of Actuaries and Faculty of Actuaries).

McGillivray, Warren R. 1992. "Actuarial aspects of converting provident funds into social insurance schemes", in Committee on Provident Funds: *Twelfth Meeting of the Committee, Reports and summaries of discussions* (Geneva, ISSA).

——. 1996. "Actuarial valuations of social security schemes: Necessity, utility and misconceptions", in ISSA, 1996.

——. 1997. *An operational framework for pension reform: Retirement system risks* (Geneva, ILO, Social Security Department; mimeographed).

Neill, Alistair. 1986. *Life contingencies* (London, Heinemann).

Picard, J.-P. 1971. "Note on a computer programme for making demographic and financial projections under a pension scheme involving survivors' benefits", in ISSA: *Proceedings of the Fifth International Conference of Social Security Actuaries and Statisticians* (Berne).

——. 1975. *Application de l'ordinateur aux projections démographiques et financières d'un régime d'assurance-pensions*, paper presented at the Sixth International Conference of Social Security Actuaries and Statisticians (Helsinki, ISSA).

——. 1979. *Le programme d'ordinateur du Bureau international du Travail pour les projections démographiques et financières des régimes de sécurité sociale*, paper presented at the Seventh International Conference of Social Security Actuaries and Statisticians (Mexico, ISSA).

——. 1996. "Valuation of the financial equilibrium of long-term benefits schemes", in ISSA, 1996.

Thullen, P. 1964. "The scaled premium system for the financing of social insurance pension schemes", in *International Review on Actuarial and Statistical Problems of Social Security*, No. 10 (Geneva, ISSA).

——. 1973. *Techniques actuarielles de la sécurité sociale* (Geneva, ILO).

Tilove, Robert. 1976. *Public employee pension funds* (New York and London, Columbia University Press).

Trowbridge, C.L.; Farr, C.E. 1976. *The theory and practice of pension funding* (Homewood, Illinois, Richard D. Irwin).

World Bank. 1994. *Averting the old age crisis: Policies to protect the old and promote growth* (New York, Oxford University Press).

Zelenka, A. 1958. "Quelques remarques sur le régime financier", in ISSA: *Actuarial and statistical problems of social security*, Vol. III (Geneva and Rome).

——. 1959. "Fonctions biométriques et économiques interchangeables dans l'équation générale de l'équilibre financier", in ISSA: *Transactions of the Second International Conference of Social Security Actuaries and Statisticians* (Geneva).

INDEX